CAMBRIDGE LIBRARY COLLECTION

*Books of enduring scholarly value*

## Women's Writing

The later twentieth century saw a huge wave of academic interest in women's writing, which led to the rediscovery of neglected works from a wide range of genres, periods and languages. Many books that were immensely popular and influential in their own day are now studied again, both for their own sake and for what they reveal about the social, political and cultural conditions of their time. A pioneering resource in this area is Orlando: Women's Writing in the British Isles from the Beginnings to the Present (http://orlando.cambridge.org), which provides entries on authors' lives and writing careers, contextual material, timelines, sets of internal links, and bibliographies. Its editors have made a major contribution to the selection of the works reissued in this series within the Cambridge Library Collection, which focuses on non-fiction publications by women on a wide range of subjects from astronomy to biography, music to political economy, and education to prison reform.

## Essays on the Pursuits of Women

Frances Power Cobbe (1822–1904) was an Irish writer, social reformer and activist best known for her contributions to Victorian feminism and women's suffrage. After the death of her father in 1857, Cobbe travelled extensively across Europe before becoming a leader-writer addressing public issues for the London newspaper The Echo in 1868. She continued to publish on the topics of feminism, social problems and theology for the rest of her life. This volume, first published in 1863, contains a series of essays discussing topics of importance to early feminists. Cobbe explores sexual and matrimonial inequality and the changing status of and opportunities for single women, and advocates greater and more extensive female education. Cobbe also discusses possible reasons behind the inequality and limitations experienced by singe and married women, providing insights into the lives experienced by Victorian women and exemplifying the ideas and concerns of contemporary feminists. For more information on this author, see http://orlando.cambridge.org/public/svPeople?person_id=cobbfr

Cambridge University Press has long been a pioneer in the reissuing of out-of-print titles from its own backlist, producing digital reprints of books that are still sought after by scholars and students but could not be reprinted economically using traditional technology. The Cambridge Library Collection extends this activity to a wider range of books which are still of importance to researchers and professionals, either for the source material they contain, or as landmarks in the history of their academic discipline.

Drawing from the world-renowned collections in the Cambridge University Library, and guided by the advice of experts in each subject area, Cambridge University Press is using state-of-the-art scanning machines in its own Printing House to capture the content of each book selected for inclusion. The files are processed to give a consistently clear, crisp image, and the books finished to the high quality standard for which the Press is recognised around the world. The latest print-on-demand technology ensures that the books will remain available indefinitely, and that orders for single or multiple copies can quickly be supplied.

The Cambridge Library Collection will bring back to life books of enduring scholarly value (including out-of-copyright works originally issued by other publishers) across a wide range of disciplines in the humanities and social sciences and in science and technology.

# Essays on the Pursuits of Women

*Also, a Paper on Female Education*

Frances Power Cobbe

CAMBRIDGE UNIVERSITY PRESS

Cambridge, New York, Melbourne, Madrid, Cape Town, Singapore,
São Paolo, Delhi, Dubai, Tokyo, Mexico City

Published in the United States of America by Cambridge University Press, New York

www.cambridge.org
Information on this title: www.cambridge.org/9781108020480



This edition first published 1863
This digitally printed version 2010

ISBN 978-1-108-02048-0 Paperback

# ESSAYS

ON THE

# PURSUITS OF WOMEN.

REPRINTED FROM

FRASER'S AND MACMILLAN'S MAGAZINES.

ALSO

## A PAPER ON FEMALE EDUCATION,

*Read before the Social Science Congress. at Guildhall.*

BY

FRANCES POWER COBBE.

LONDON:

EMILY FAITHFULL,

*Printer and Publisher in Ordinary to Her Majesty,*

PRINCES STREET, HANOVER SQUARE, AND 83A, FARRINGDON STREET.

1863.

TO MY THREE DEAR AND HONOURED FRIENDS,

THE AUTHORESS OF

"THE CONNECTION OF THE PHYSICAL SCIENCES,"

THE FOUNDRESS OF

THE FIRST FEMALE REFORMATORY,

AND

THE SCULPTRESS OF "ZENOBIA,"

I DEDICATE THIS BOOK,

ON THE PURSUITS OF WOMEN.

FRANCES POWER COBBE.

# PREFACE.

THREE Essays in this volume—the second, third, and fourth—constitute a connected series; the remainder are of a miscellaneous character, and were written at various times, and for different purposes more or less nearly allied to the general subject of the Pursuits of Women. No pretension is made in them to any adequate treatment of so large a theme, but only to the discussion of a few of the lines lately opened to women's interests and employments of the more intellectual kind. Especially do these little Essays apply to the pursuits of *Single* women—of those who, being debarred from the most natural and blessed of human ties and duties, yet believe that the lives which it has pleased God to bestow on them should neither be aimless for themselves, nor valueless for His creatures.

CLIFTON,

*March*, 1863.

# CONTENTS.

# ESSAY I.

## SOCIAL SCIENCE CONGRESSES, AND WOMEN'S PART IN THEM.

*Reprinted from Macmillan's Magazine, December*, 1861.

"CURE the world by *science!*" said an irate old gentleman to us this year in Dublin. "Don't talk to me of your Social *Science!* Make people read their Bibles, and teach their children, and keep their houses clean, and attend to their business instead of the alehouse; but don't talk balderdash about Social Science! Science indeed! *Social* Science! pshaw!"

Vain would it have been, no doubt, to try to persuade that excellent practical philanthropist that, like M. Jourdain, who had been "talking prose all his life without ever suspecting it," so he had been similarly studying Social Science; and that it even takes no small share of the same to teach people all the good things he desired. Equally hopeless would it be to argue with one who should question whether the evils of pauperism, crime, and vice were more likely to be cured by chance and isolated efforts, than by the intelligent method and co-operation of persons devoted to the task, and studying, *as a science*, the solemn problems of human misery, and its possible relief. The late meeting in Dublin of the Association for the Promotion of Social Science may be counted so definitely a success, as to establish the right of such congresses to be ranked among the more prominent institutions of our times. We think ourselves accordingly fully justified in inviting our readers to a careful consideration of the various aspects of such meetings, and their probable bearings on our present condition and future prospects.

At the first blush, it is obvious that there are in them many points of unquestionable hopefulness and promise. We cannot engage to discuss the subject from the empyrean heights of wholly uninterested criticism. We feel, on the contrary, somewhat puzzled to conceive the mental state of the man who can do so; who witnesses without one glow of human sympathy so many persons assembled from every part of the kingdom, and even from distant countries, with the one recognised object of contributing what may lie in their power towards the common cause of "peace on earth, and good-will to man." Only in our age could such a purpose serve to collect such an assembly. *War*, indeed, has its councils, even among Caffres and Mohawks. The impenetrable mysteries of scholastic theology have called a thousand synods to determine the most recondite secrets of our great Maker's nature. Physical science, art, and literature have had their academies and institutions beyond numbering, in modern Europe. But it was reserved for the later half of our century to find even a name for that pursuit which directly tries to make mankind more good and happy, and fulfil, as best they may, the second great commandment in the Law. The mistakes, the failures, the displays of human folly and weakness (if such there should appear) at a congress like this, would make a lover of his kind rather inclined to grieve than to laugh, to lament any defect in a noble work rather than to glory over the weakness displayed by the workers.

On the other hand, there are some pertinent questions to be asked, and, perhaps, doubts to be entertained, respecting the existing mode of conducting these assemblies. We confess that on the face of it the idea is rather alarming of a large association of ladies and gentlemen, enjoying rights of membership on the qualification of a small subscription, and meeting together annually to read wholly independent and disjointed lucubrations, which, unless quite inadmissible in their character, the courteous secretary will hardly be willing to reject. That section of the community whose office in the social machine is that of the drag, and who unfortunately perform their functions whenever it is going *up* hill no less than down —these good persons have not failed to fasten themselves tightly on this new wheel of progress. "In every other science," they remark, "some period of apprenticeship is admitted to be necessary. But Social Science would appear to be a Minerva, springing fully armed out of the head of Jupiter. People are ready-made 'sociologists' the moment they have taught a child, or sent a thief to jail, or given tea to an old woman. Nay, they need not have practically done so much as this. They may have evolved some gigantic scheme for the benefit of the universe merely, like the celebrated 'idea' of the camel, 'out of the depths of their moral consciousness,' and in the high regions of Social Science they may disport them at their own sweet will, almost as it were in vacuo. It is nearly as good as being clergymen, to be able to preach (though it be but for twenty minutes), and to know that nobody can contradict them. The audience may, indeed, applaud, but the laws of Social Science utterly forbid all sibilation." In other words, it is manifestly absurd to expect that any good can come of meetings so constituted.

We shall endeavour, if possible, to obtain a correct idea of what Social Science itself purposes to be, what are its legitimate objects and necessary limitations. Then we shall briefly describe the past history and present condition of the Association for the promotion of this science; and, lastly, offer such replies as may seem just to the more prominent objections brought against it from various quarters.

The debate, whether Morals properly form a deductive or an inductive science, has occupied some of the greatest minds of the world. Do we obtain the laws of social and personal duty from certain principles implanted by our Creator in our natures; or must we seek for them among the experienced results of actions upon the happiness or misery of ourselves and mankind? Are we to *deduce* from the intuitive axiomatic principles of "Love thy neighbour," and "Be perfect," the remoter propositions which are to determine our special obligations, or are we to *induce* from the largest attainable basis of experience the generalizations which we may then erect into canons of morality? On the one side (that of ethics being independent of the happiness test) we have a grand array of noble names—Plato and Zeno, Aristotle, Cicero, Seneca, Antoninus, Chrysostom, St. Bernard, Abelard, Cudworth, Jeremy Taylor, Shaftesbury, Clarke, Balguy, Hutcheson, South, Law, Fichte, and the two greatest moralists of any age—Bishop Butler and Immanuel Kant. And on the other side (that of ethics being the result of experience) we have another array, yet hardly of such names as on the former roll—Epicurus, Aristippus, Democritus, Machiavelli, Pomponatius, Gassendi, Sharrock, Cumberland, Locke, Grotius, Puffendorf, Paley, Bentham, and the one great living champion, John Stuart Mill. Again, on the one hand, different theories have been propounded respecting the origin, nature, and limits of the Intuitive or Innate Ideas, or Moral Sense of right and wrong. On the other hand, the nature of the happiness test, and the persons who are to enjoy the same, are most variously stated. It may be either the εὐθυμία, the intrinsic happiness of the *mens conscia recti*, to be found in virtue itself, which we are (according to Democritus, Cumberland, and More) to note and follow; or it may be the ἡδονή, the mere "pleasure" of Aristippus; or the εὐδαιμονία, the general "felicity," present or future, of Epicurus or Paley. And, again, we may apply ourselves to the discovery of what will give *us*, individually, such pleasure or happiness here or hereafter; or we may merge our own interests in that of the mass of mankind, and inquire only what will produce "the greatest happiness of the greatest number." This last doctrine (so different from the selfish system of Paley, and illustrated with such power by Bentham and Mill) stands at this moment as the sole surviving representation of the inductive school of morals. Its lesson is even ostentatiously lucid—"Obtain from statistics the largest possible basis of facts, the most extensive accumulation of results of actions on the happiness of the community, and then induce therefrom the laws which, when so obtained, must be accounted to possess the sanctity of moral obligations."

We have been thus explicit in stating the great ethical problem, because we believe that a misapprehension exists as to the relation of Social Science to this controversy. It is supposed that all researches into the conditions of public welfare necessarily imply that we consider the results so obtained as ultimate principles of morals, beyond which there is no higher sanction of duty. Thus those to whom the names of Plato, Butler, and Kant, convey an impression not to be shared by Democritus, Paley, and Bentham, are unjustly prejudiced against a science which, in truth, involves no such concession. "What other view, then, can we hold?" Why, simply this—

The nature of all exact science is to teach us *abstract* universal principles. It cannot possibly descend below these to practical applications. By geometry I learn that a triangle is equal to half a rectangle under the same base and altitude, but no geometry can teach me whether one of my fields be a triangle with equal base and altitude with the adjoining rectangle. To know this I must see and measure them, and then geometry will tell me that the one contains half as many acres as the other. Likewise in morals, intuition teaches me the axiom that I must love my neighbour, and reflection will deduce the proposition that I must relieve the wants of the poor to the best of my ability. But no deductive science of morals can teach me what are the wants of John Styles, nor whether he will be best relieved by alms or by employment. Where deductive science stops, the inductive one must meet it, and, by a process which modern logicians have named traduction, we pass from one order of reasoning to another, and complete a science of ethics practically applicable to every detail of life.

But because induction has this great work to do, because the field which experience is to measure is of vast extent, because we need it to show us *how* to obey the moral law in our hearts, not therefore must it be mistaken for that law itself. Because it has taught us how to confer happiness on our neighbour, it must not set up happiness as the sole end of morality; because it has advised our benevolence what is expedient, it must not make benevolence a matter of expediency. Let the experimentalist, by all means, teach us how to educate the masses, but let him not ask the utility of enlarging the capacity for virtue in rational souls. Let him teach us how to emancipate the slave but let him not dare to question whether restoring to one-sixth of a community the rights of manhood will, on the whole, conduce to "the greatest happiness of the greatest number."

We believe the utilitarian system to be philosophically untenable and morally paralysing to the energies of all save the noblest souls. Therefore we repudiate all imaginary connexion between it and Social Science, and maintain that though it is the office of such science to supply the experimental basis of facts on which the moral law is to take effect, yet it appeals for its impulse of duty and its divine sanction to a very different principle, namely, to "the law written on the hearts" of all men, whether Jew or Gentile,

> "The unwritten Law Divine,
> Immutable, eternal, not like these of yesterday,
> But made ere time began." *

The province, then, of Social Science, as we would understand it, is simple enough. At the present stage our task is nearly the same as that which Bacon commenced for physical science in the *Novum Organon.* In the first place, a vast accumulation of facts and observations, statistics and experiments, need to be gathered and constated. Then out of these, gradually, by induction, larger generalizations will be reached, one principle after another will be ascertained, and the laws regulating public health, crime, pauperism, &c., will be discovered. It is obviously impossible at first to know where exactly to look for the more important facts, and to choose among those presented to us only such as may be of permanent value. We must be content to act like a geologist at a quarry, and be satisfied, though the workmen bring many worthless stones along with some precious fossils, out of which, by and by, may be framed a form of life and beauty all unseen hitherto by mortal eyes. The *general* benefits of the whole scheme may be summed up as follows.

* Sophocles, *Antigone*, 454.

Of the *particular* practical achievements we will speak by and by.

1. The science itself is advanced by the accumulation, comparison, and verification of the discoveries of the leading students year by year, the facts they have noted, and the experiments they have made.

2. Individual students receive instruction and encouragement each from each, and are further immensely aided in carrying out their special tasks by acquaintance with all others similarly engaged in the kingdom, whose work and their own henceforth proceed with mutual co-operation.

3. Persons not hitherto occupied in practical philanthropy acquire an interest in one or other branch of the subject, and thenceforth give their influence, time, or money to the cause.

4. The Legislature receives with respect the opinions and advice of those who have made these matters their study, because they are now presented, not as isolated views of individuals, but as the deliberate resolutions of a large and respectable body of thinkers and workers.

In a word, the principle of associated action, whose adoption Channing so well described as one of the most distinguishing characteristics of our century, and one of the most powerful of future agencies in the world, is now applied to the promotion, not merely of war, nor commerce, nor the abstruse controversies of theology; not merely to the advancement of physical or mathematical science, of arts, or of literature; but directly and immediately to the promotion of the virtue and happiness of the human race. Social Science aims to embrace every department of the vast field wherein must be waged the warfare of Ormuzd against Ahrimanes, virtue against vice, innocence against crime, health against disease, knowledge against ignorance, peace against war, industry against pauperism, and woman against the degradation of her sex. No wonder that the mockers sneer at the immensity of the undertaking, as they did when the education of the poor was attempted twenty years ago, and the jest ran on the efforts to convey the "rudiments of omniscience" through a Penny Magazine. It *is* a gigantic science, that of the laws which govern human society. It is an enterprise almost hopeless in its magnitude, to attempt to cope with the sin and misery of the world, and, like Kehama, storm the citadel of evil on all sides, and drive at once,

"Self-multiplied, down all the roads of Padalon."

He who would say that the labours of twenty such associations in a dozen years could actually accomplish any one department of the task, would "talk Utopian;" but not the less must we wish God-speed to a plan which promises to do more than a thousand *isolated* workers have done or could do in centuries.

The first beginning of the Social Science congresses may be traced to a small meeting of persons interested in the reformatory movement, at Hardwick Court, in Gloucestershire, the seat of Mr. Barwick Baker, in the autumn of 1855. Before separating on this occasion, the members of the meeting formed themselves into a society, under the name of the National Reformatory Union.

In August, 1856, the society held at Bristol its first provincial meeting; which, in all respects, resembled those of the present congresses, except that subjects connected with crime and reformation were the only ones discussed in the sections. The extended interest excited by the proceedings of this provincial meeting suggested naturally that a still wider field of discussion should be opened. At the next assemblage, at Birmingham, in October, 1857, the "National Reformatory Union" merged in the "Association for the Promotion of Social Science," under the auspices of Lord Brougham. The second congress of the new society took place in Liverpool, in 1858, the third at Bradford, in 1859, the fourth at Glasgow, in 1860, and the fifth and last in Dublin, in 1861. On each occasion, the numbers both of speakers and audience at the meetings have shown a large increase, till the congresses have assumed their present proportions, and the vast halls of the

Dublin Four Courts were not more than sufficient to contain the throngs of members and associates.*

It may now be fitly asked, What work has been done by this new and gigantic machine? The answer is not far to seek. Of course a large share of the results of such meetings are of those *general* kinds which we have already indicated, and which cannot be reduced to definite statements, although we may form some judgment of their magnitude by the rise in the barometer of public opinion on all matters connected with the objects of the Association when treated by the press. It is a very few years ago since the *Morning Post* gave it as its opinion that one of the ablest heads in England was unquestionably cracked, because the owner stood foremost among the advocates for the reformation of juvenile criminals. We should be rather surprised, in 1861, to find the labours of the Recorder of Birmingham thus treated even in journals remarkable for antiquity, both of date and of sentiment. A tone of contemptuous compassion was generally adopted towards those "whose charity outran their discretion," and who were weak enough to believe that their fellow-creatures might be reclaimed from crime and pauperism. As to the lower class of journals, they merely sneered and jested, and hinted at the vanity and love

* Since these pages were written, the Congress in London of 1862 has carried the Association many steps forward. Nearly all the special labours presently to be described, have importantly advanced in the past year.

of notoriety which are well known to underlie all philanthropy. Perhaps we have some vestiges of this bygone folly in some quarters yet; but the general tone is immensely altered. Those who first rowed hard against the stream of public feeling now find it carrying them forward with its tide.

But the Social Science Association does not lack specific achievements to allege in its own behalf, as well as general utility. In the first place, the whole legislation of the last few years on the subject of crime has been importantly influenced by its action. This last summer, in Dublin, the greatest achievement of all has been accomplished by the public recognition of Captain Crofton's Intermediate Convict System, as the only one which has ever successfully coped in this country with the problem of reforming adult criminals, and the consequent re-establishment of its founder in the post which he was on the point of quitting, in despair, to the probable ruin of his undertaking. Not only for Ireland is this beneficent plan now permanently secured, but we have every reason to anticipate, ere long, its adoption in this country, since a deputation of several eminent Yorkshire magistrates and members of Parliament have been induced, from the results of the congress, to go over to Dublin on purpose to examine the practical working of the system, and have returned amply satisfied of its excellence.

Baron Holzendorff, one of the members of the

Association, has already obtained its establishment in Prussia.

Much has also been effected by the Association, more or less directly, towards various other legal reforms—the consolidation of the Criminal Law, the improvement of International and of Quarantine Laws, Sir W. Page Wood's reforms respecting Charitable Trusts, the amendments in the Bankruptcy and Insolvency Laws, the Repeal of the Paper Duty, and many other movements in the right direction. The volume entitled "Trades' Societies and Strikes" embodies the results of two years' labour by a committee of the Association. It has become the standard work on the subject, and we cannot doubt it will be of vast benefit in arresting those disturbances of trade which have caused such misery to thousands, merely from their ignorance of social laws. The cause of Education, as Lord Brougham remarked at the last congress, has gained many advantages from the Association. The formation of co-operative societies, of which two hundred and fifty have been enrolled in the last twelvemonths, is another branch of progress.

Again, there are three subsidiary societies, all working in connexion with the Social Science Association, and vastly indebted to it for support. The Ladies' Sanitary Association circulates admirable tracts, and has lectures delivered in the poorer dis tricts of London and throughout the country, instructing the people, and especially mothers, on those natural laws on whose observance the health of the community immediately depends. The Society for the Employment of Women has apprenticed girls to the Victoria Printing Press, introduced women to the law copying trade, and is now actively prosecuting a scheme for the safe emigration of that most piteous class on whom the evils of woman's helplessness fall heaviest—women above the rank of servants, yet unable to earn their bread in England by any other industry. From an admirable paper, read by Miss Parkes on the subject, at the congress, we are enabled to guess at the immensity of the want to be thus supplied. "A short time since, 810 women applied for one situation of £15 per annum, and 250 for another worth only £12." A branch of this Society has been formed, at the late congress, for Ireland. Lastly, the Workhouse Visiting Society, affiliated from the first to the Social Science Association, is also doing its work. Upwards of a hundred workhouses are now regularly visited, which, a few years ago, rarely received a drop from the plentiful spring of English charity, poured so freely on all save these most miserable paupers! Miss L. Twining's Home for the Instruction of Workhouse Girls has, we trust, in its present seventeen inmates, the beginnings of a scheme which, adopted through the country, shall rescue these girls from the present system, which has made the hard and heartless workhouse school one of the widest channels into the abyss of woman's degradation. Miss Elliot, daughter of the Dean of Bristol, in starting the scheme for separate wards, with admission of voluntary charity, for the incurables, has worked already the relief of many hundreds of the most wretched of God's creatures. This last year, in Dublin, the meeting of the congress in that city awoke the interest and secured the entrance of a committee of ladies to the great South Dublin Union, where 1,400 sick are now blessing their presence. "It would be difficult," said the president, "to overrate the importance of the reform of workhouses, or the merits of Miss Twining, whose care and time and great abilities have long been devoted to the subject."

But it is beyond our knowledge or power to enumerate the different and sometimes unexpected lines in which the action of the Association goes forward. Let us take one illustration more, and then leave the subject. At the congress of 1858, Mr. C. Melly read a paper, describing the fountains which he had erected in Liverpool, with the happiest effect in lessening the prevailing drunkenness. The Council allowed a separate edition of the tract, with the print of the fountain as a model, to be published; and it was extensively distributed during the congress. "The effect has been to spread the establishment of fountains over the whole country; and it is certain that the benefit thus derived has been owing to the services of the Association." (Lord Brougham's Address, 1859.)

Our next step ought naturally to be, after specifying the merits of the Social Science Association, to add some statement of the objections, real or fictitious, urged against it. This is, however, we avow, a most alarming task. There is a sort of generalization about these objections which renders it by no means easy to express them in words. First, there is the name itself. One most able journal actually asserted that there was not, and could not be, such a thing as Social Science at all; thereby reducing the Association very much to the character of schemers in the South Sea Bubble! Far larger is that portion of the public who recalcitrate at once at the thing and the name, for the simple reason that both are new. "Sociology" is the sort of thing the Sorbonne would have condemned as "*mal-sonnant et sentant d'hérésie.*" It conveys nearly the same unpleasant feelings to the mind as those direful compounds "Neology," "Anthropomorphism," "Subjectivity," and the like. And then, has it not something to do with that French system—what is it called?—"Socialism?" He who thinks such ideas as these can have no real influence, knows very little of the power of folly in the world.

A much more serious objection is that to which we have already partly referred—namely, the enormous magnitude of the field of operations, and the wholly irregular action of the forces. We admit that immense difficulties must, doubtless, lie a-head in the way of the Secretary and Council to organize and select the papers and speeches as year after year they multiply, so as to prevent the time of the meetings being wasted by indifferent contributions, while securing all those worthy of attention. As the heap of quartz grows larger it will be more and more difficult to extract all the gold. However, the world has little right to question the further wisdom of guidance hitherto so successful; and, perhaps, the utmost sagacity which can be shown in the case will be to follow Mrs. Browning's advice to the poet—

"Keep up the fire,
And leave the generous flames to shape themselves."

The most successful, however, of all the attacks of our witty contemporaries on the Social Science Association, are those which refered to the very considerable part taken therein by ladies; and to this, therefore, we shall devote the residue of our space.

There is a whole mine of jokes to be found at all times by the destitute in the subject of woman. Readers may remain in unmoved gravity while *men*, however absurd or ridiculous, are the subject of sarcasm; but *women!*—"Law, master," as Diggory says, "you must not tell me the story of the grouse in the gun-room, for, if you do, I *must* laugh." A silly old woman in a mob cap, or a silly young one in a crinoline, a Belgravian mother, or a "pretty horsebreaker," women who know Greek, and women who cannot spell English, ladies who do nothing but crochet, and ladies who write two hundred letters a day for Borrioboola Gha—it is pretty much the same; who can resist the fun of the thing, even if it be repeated rather frequently? Frankly we confess, for our own parts, that, while reason tells us the joke is rather superannuated, habit still induces us to enjoy it as ever fresh and new.

We do, indeed, sometimes figure to ourselves the employer (we cannot say originator) of such a jest as a person not naturally of a lively disposition, but rather as one whom the requirements of a despotic editor compel sometimes to become jovial—one who has a "*concern*" to be diverting; who is witty, not so much by nature as by grace. We hear him crying in his extreme distress, "What shall I do to be funny? Who will show me any joke? *Date obolum Belisario!*" At last a blessed thought occurs to him, "We will stand on the old paths and see which were the ancient jests." And there, of course, in the first page of the first book he opens, from Aristophanes to Joe Miller, he finds a jibe at women. "Eureka!" exclaims the fortunate man; "why, of course, the women! That is always sure to succeed with the galleries." With a skip and a bound, and a sommersault, amazing to beholders, the solemn critic comes out a first-rate clown. "All right!" "Here we are!" "At them again!"

Of course it is a double piece of good fortune when (as on the occasion of the holding of the late congress in Dublin) Penseroso in search of a Joke lights upon it in Ireland. One might almost indeed suspect that his necessities had driven him in that particular quarter, as Shakspeare says, "to taste the subtleties of the Isle!" The very dullest of Englishmen can always find a laugh for stories of Irish beggars, Irish bulls, and Irish cars. Possibly it may chance to be because he *is* dull that the quickness and brightness of the Irish mind strikes him as so amazing. He feels much like one of the hard-fisted *habitués* of an ale-house gazing at the rapid fingering of the fiddler. "Do look at un's hands how fast they go! Could'ee do the likes of that, man? Haw, haw, haw!" No other nation that we know of considers it so strange to be able to answer a simple question with vivacity, and to elaborate a joke in less than half an hour.

But to return to the women. A peculiar merit of the Protean joke against them is that it accommodates itself immediately to every new line of action which they may adopt. And, as in our day, women are continually adopting new lines of action, the supply for the jest market seems really inexhaustible.

We would not on any account be discourteous to the sex; but yet we cannot help sometimes comparing them in our minds to a large flock of sheep, round which some little worrying terriers, with ears erect and outstretched tails, are barking and jumping, (occasionally) biting in a wholly facetious manner. The foolish sheep run hither and thither; but, whichever way they go, the terriers hunt them out of *that* corner immediately. Now they rush into this thicket —now down into that ditch—now out again into the open field. Here are two sheep running away on one side, there is another going off in the opposite direction. "Bow, wow, wow!" cry the little dogs. "Bow, wow, wow! Don't go here—don't go there—don't separate yourselves—don't run together. Bow, wow, wow, wow!" At last the idiotic sheep (any one of whom might have knocked down the little terrier quite easily if it only had the pluck) go rushing, like the demoniacal swine, down into the very worst hole they can possibly find; and then the little dogs give a solemn growl, and drop their tails, and return home in great moral indignation.

We are for ever hearing of women's proper work being this, that, or the other. But, whatever they actually undertake, it is always clear that *that* is not the "mission" in question; they must run off and try some other corner directly. In the days of our grandmothers it was the frivolity of the Delias and Narcissas which was the theme of satire—

> "A youth of follies, an old age of cards,"

was the head and front of their offending. It was a subject of scorn, that "most women have no character at all," and that while

> "*Men*, some to business, some to pleasure take,
> Yet every *woman* is at heart a rake."

The "tea-cup age" passed away, and the sheep rushed in an opposite direction. Women would be frivolous no more. They became "Blues!"—and the barking went on worse than ever! It was thought the wittiest thing in the world for Byron to sneer at his noble wife (who has so lately closed her life of honour, silent to the last regarding all *his* offences!) because she was

> "A learned lady, famed
> For every branch of every science known,
> In every Christian language ever named,
> With virtues equalled by her wit alone."

Efforts were made at the time to give young ladies, generally, an education which should transcend the wretched *curriculum* of the then fashionable schools—"French, the guitar, and Poonah painting," with "history, geography, and the use of the globes," thrown into the bargain as unimportant items. Then it was the acquirement of knowledge which was *not* "woman's mission," and which would infallibly distract her from it. It was supposed that "a mother's solicitude for her children depended on her ignorance of Greek and mathematics; and that she would be likely to desert an infant for a quadratic equation." Those phrases which Sydney Smith called the "delight of Noodledom" were in continual circulation. "The true theatre for a woman is the sick chamber." "The only thing a woman need know is how to take care of children; that is what she was *made for*, and there is no use attempting to overstep the intentions of nature."

But of late a most singular transition has taken place. The sheep are running, it would seem, precisely where the terriers were driving them. The care of the sick and of children occupies the minds and lives of great numbers of women who have few or no domestic duties. Let us see how they are treated by the little dogs. Alas! we fear that we catch the sound of the bark again. Ladies must not meddle with this school. Ladies must not interfere with that hospital. Ladies ought not to give evidence before committees of Parliament. Ladies cannot be admitted into workhouses. Ladies ought not to make a stir about the grievances they discover. Ladies ought not to write papers about paupers, and women's employment, and children's education. And oh! above all earthly things, ladies ought not to read such papers, even if they write them. "Bow, wow, wow, wow!" They must (we are driven to conclude) nurse the sick without meddling in schools, and see evils but never publish them, and write (if they *must* write) papers about babies and girls, and then get some man to read the same (of course losing the entire pith and point thereof) while they sit by, dumb and "diffident," rejoicing in the possession of tongues and voices which, of course, it cannot have been "the intention of nature" should ever be heard appealing in their feminine softness for pity and help for the ignorant and the suffering.

Now, we confess, in all seriousness, to be rather tired of this kind of thing. It seems to us that the world does grievously need the aid of one half the human race to mitigate the evils which oppress it; and if, in their early and feeble endeavours to fulfil their share of the work, women should make endless blunders, the error in our eyes is a venial one, compared to the inactivity and uselessness in which (in Protestant countries) so many of them habitually vegetate. Let us not be mistaken. The private and home duties of *such women as have them* are, beyond all doubt, their first concern, and one which, when fully met, must often engross all their time and energies. But it is an absurdity, peculiar to the treatment of women, to go on assuming that all of them *have* home duties, and tacitly treating those who have none as if they were wrongly placed on God's earth, and had nothing whatever to do in it. There must needs be a purpose for the lives of single women in the social order of Providence—a definite share in the general system which they are intended to carry on. The Church of Rome found out this truth long ago. The Catholic woman who does not marry, takes it almost as a matter of course that she is bound to devote herself to works of general charity and piety. While the Protestant "old maid" has been for centuries among the most wretched and useless of human beings—all her nature dwindled by restraint, and the affections, which might have cheered many a sufferer, centred on a cat or a parrot—the Romanist has understood that she has *not* fewer duties than others, but more extended and perhaps laborious ones. Not selfishness—gross to a proverb—but self-sacrifice more entire than belongs to the double life of marriage, is the true law of celibacy. Doubtless it is not an easy law. It will take some time to learn the lesson; for it is far harder to preserve a loving spirit in solitude than under the fostering warmth of sweet household affections. If the single woman allows herself to drift down the stream of circumstances, making no effort for better things, then the shoals of selfishness lie inevitably beneath the prow. To row against the tide of inclination more vigorously than others, to seek resolutely for distant duties when no near ones present themselves, to give more love while receiving less—such are the stern claims of duty on a lonely woman.

But, now that she is beginning to feel somewhat of these solemn obligations, that hundreds and even thousands of women of the upper classes are saying, "What shall I do with my life? for neither balls, nor crochet, nor novels, nor *dilettante* copying of drawings and playing of music, satisfy my soul, and I would fain do some little fraction of good before I die"—shall we *now* spend our wit in trying to warn them off such fields as they may try to work, instead of helping them with all manly sense and tenderness? "Women are invading the province of men. They are not our equals, and they have no business to do it." If the inferiority be so definite, the alarm is at least very groundless. We should not, I think, have raised the Volunteers, if it were the inhabitants of Madagascar who threatened to invade England. Let a woman's powers be set down to the lowest figure imaginable; let it be assumed (a tolerably large assumption!) that the most clear-headed and warm-hearted woman is the inferior in all respects of the most consummate masculine "muff" of her acquaintance, and that she ought to listen in humility and prostration of mind whenever he opens his lips (for the unanswerable reason that a moustache may grow upon them), still, with Herbert Spencer, we must ask, "Is it any reason, because a woman's powers are inferior, that she should be prevented from using such powers as she *has?*"

We are not going to descend into that miserable arena of controversy, the question of the equality of men and women. To us, individually, it seems that the combatants have usually been about as wise as if they debated whether railway shares and the north star, a sonata by Beethoven and the *Wellingtonia gigantea*, were equal to one another. "Equality" is a word which hardly applies to moral and spiritual creatures at all. No two men are equal to one another in all ways—hardly in *any* way we can name, except in purely physical qualities of height, and weight, and strength.

But the *equivalency* of men and women is a very different question from their *equality;* and here it seems to us there is much to be learned from a fair consideration of the relative gifts divided (roughly speaking) between the sexes. There are many points on which most men are superior to most women. There are others (it can hardly be denied) in which most women are superior to most men. If these latter be on the whole as valuable points (if not as obtrusive ones) as the others, then there is a real *equivalency,* albeit not in one particular is there equality.

In plain language, we hold that the one is the pound in gold, the other the twenty shillings in silver. More nicely speaking, the man is the gold sovereign, nearly everywhere and always at par. The woman is a pound cheque, which may or may not be payable to the bearer. The whole obscurity of the question has arisen from this—that the peculiar value of woman is not by any means always to be produced. It never comes out in full save under conditions so favourable that as yet the world has but rarely offered them. The relation of equivalency which a cultivated and religious English or American lady bears to her well-matched husband, is one which has few parallels in other ranks, or lands, or ages. And the reason is clear. The bodily strength, the powerful understanding, the sound moral sense, the creative powers of man, can all secure, more or less, their development. But the delicate physical beauty, the brilliant intuitions, the refined taste, the tender conscience, the loving piety, and the self-forgetting affections of women, as imperatively need an atmosphere of confidence and refinement in which to expand, as the *Victoria regia* needs warm and quiet waters in which to blossom.

But all this is in truth beside the mark.

A man has had his left arm bound up in a sling for many years. It is, no doubt, very stiff from disuse, very feeble, and at best a left hand, not a right one. The man at last bethinks him, "I declare I will take my left hand out of this sling; true, it is very little good—still there is a great deal I cannot do with my right hand alone." Would it not be rather absurd if a friend should suggest, "Don't do anything of the kind; your right hand can do everything much better by itself. As to the left (though it *has* five fingers too) it is meant for nothing but to hang in that sling round your neck. *Nature obviously never intended anything else.*" We believe that this same *left hand* of humanity is grievously wanted to do some of the world's work. Not, indeed, to do the right hand's part, but its own; to help in as perfect and needful co-operation as the two limbs of the same individual. Few signs of the future seem to us more promising than this, that the left hand is coming out of the sling—that women are putting themselves, however feebly and awkwardly at first, to their proper tasks. It is assuredly a topic of deep interest to *all*, both men and women. How can this unused hand be brought into activity? We are not going to dilate on women's

> "Particular worth and general missionariness:"

but we think the following are some of the points in which their help is needed at this time.

We want, in the first place, the Religious and Moral intuitions of women to be brought out so as to complete those of men, to give us all that *stereoscopic view* by which we shall see such truths as we can never see them by single vision, however clear and strong. Old Iamblichus tells us that "the genius of women is most adapted to piety," and traces the aphorism to "the wisest of all others," Thoth, or Hermes Trismegistus.* The ancient Germans, as Tacitus tells us, thought their women could approach nearer to the Deity than themselves. In all ages the piety of females has been noted. And why? Doubtless because their gentler natures and more retired lives peculiarly fit them to receive in their unruffled hearts the breath of the Divine love, and listen to that inner voice too often unheard amid the clamour of the world. We come nearer to God through the affections, wherein lie woman's great power, than through the intellect wherein man excels. It is not the marble palace mind of the philosopher which God will visit so often

* Iamblichus. De Vita Pythag. c. xi.

as the humble heart which lies sheltered from the storms of passion, and all trailed over by the fragrant blossoms of sweet human affections. Yet all the light which the Divine Spirit has surely shed on so many thousands of pious women's hearts has almost been suffered to die away without illuminating further than the narrowest circle around them. We hardly any of us know what is the spontaneous religious sentiment of woman; for, when developed hitherto, it has been nearly always under the distorting influence of some monstrous creed imposed on her uncultivated understanding. We have had enough of *man's* thoughts of God—of God first as the King, the "Man of War," the Demiurge, the Mover of all things, and then, at last, since Christian times, of God as the Father of the World. Not always have men been very competent to teach even this side of the truth alone; for during more than a thousand years the religious teachers of Christendom were men who knew not a father's feelings, who thought them not less holy than their own loveless celibacy. But the woman's thought of God as the "Parent of Good, Almighty," who unites in one the father's care and the mother's tenderness, *that* we have never yet heard. Even a woman hardly dares to trust her own heart, and believe that as she "would have compassion on the son of her womb," so the Lord hath pity on us all. Surely, surely, it is time we gain something from woman of her Religious nature! And we want her

Moral intuition also. We want her sense of the law of love to complete man's sense of the law of justice. We want her influence, inspiring virtue by gentle promptings from within to complete man's external legislation of morality. And, then, we want woman's practical service. We want her genius for detail, her tenderness for age and suffering, her comprehension of the wants of childhood to complete man's gigantic charities and nobly planned hospitals and orphanages. How shall we get at all these things?

There are, of course, endless ways in which this may be done, and, thank God, is doing at last. Each woman helps it who takes her part in the labours of poor schools and asylums, of hospitals and visiting the sick, and in the beautiful duties of a country gentleman's wife or daughter among her natural dependents. Still larger is her sphere, if she can write the thoughts of her heart. Books like Mrs. Stowe's are each worth ten or twenty lives of philanthropic labours. Is there yet any other way? Can woman's influence ever come to us otherwise than in private conversation—in her visible work—and in her written book? It is an inquiry of much interest.

The truth is unquestionable, that the most ordinary human voice conveys a power over the emotions far greater than the same ideas would bring by writing. The presence of the individual who addresses us, his whole personality brought before us—face, figure, voice, motion—are immense levers of our feelings of sympathy. No *written* or printed words have half the power of the same words spoken by their author J. D. Morell would explain the mystery philosophically. He tells us, "the nerve of the eye is nearer to the frontal region of the brain, and, being more nearly allied to the intellectual organs, it is calculated to convey impressions which appeal at once to the understanding. The nerve of the ear is nearer to the cerebellum, and is more allied to the region of passion and sentiment. Thus it is calculated to appeal rather to the *feelings and emotions* of our nature." (Psychology, p. 113.) "Sight," says Erdmann, "is the *clearest*, hearing the *deepest* of our senses."

The question whether this power ought ever to be used by women in the way in which it is most efficacious, namely, as addressing a number of persons at once, is not one to be decided too hastily. If the woman choose a subject belonging especially to men's concerns; if she fail to bring forward something worth hearing; if her manner be dictatorial or presumptuous, laying down the law like a man, instead of appealing for it like a woman; if she have too feeble a voice to be heard, or too great nervousness to speak aloud; in all these cases, we feel, she is in the wrong place. And still more decidedly do we feel that in no arena of angry debate—no position in which, *if she were a man*, she must expect to meet public disapprobation and contention—has she any right to be. In reality, nothing can be more ungenerous than the act of a woman by which she provokes opposition and disapproval as a man might do, and then appeals for defence and consideration as a woman. But do the opponents of feminine public speaking wholly forget that by far the larger part of the addresses to which we all listen are made by *men* under circumstances which more effectually preclude reply, opposition, and the expression of disapproval, than we can require to guard even the silliest lady-orators? Do not the clergy of all denominations read to us, or speak to us, from their pulpits, in the enjoyment of the most sublime immunity from the chance of a groan or an ironical cheer, a reply that "that fact is not true," or, "that argument is good for nothing?" Who will venture to affirm that, in the matters of morals and philanthropy to which we expect the addresses of women to be devoted, the same immunity enjoyed by the parsons may not be productive of, at least as much benefit? Seriously, we think that a confusion is constantly made between two sorts of public speaking. One is *argumentative*, and the other *appealing and exhortative*. For public meetings, where lines of associated action are to be decided on, nothing can be more needful and appropriate than the argumentative address; but, that it should be of use, it is imperative that there be liberty of reply and refutation. The rule is clear. The speaker to whom no reply can be made, ought never to speak *as if it could*. He loses the immense advantages of the exhortative address, and (unless in the case of persons fully convinced beforehand of every point of his argument) it is a million to one if he can satisfy anybody. All this applies to woman's public addresses in this way. If the chivalry of men make it impossible for them to contend on equal terms with women, then women have no right to challenge such contention. It would be as wrong as for a gentleman to challenge to a boxing-match a sturdy yeoman, who honoured him too much to give him a downright blow. Women, therefore, should always consider any address they may make, as essentially an *appeal*—and not an argument.

In conclusion, we can only say, for certain purposes and under such limitations as we have specified, it does appear to us that the occasional addresses of women, read or spoken, may become an agency of some value in bringing about that end which every rational man must earnestly desire, namely, the introduction of the feminine element to its full place in the moral and religious feeling of the future. Whether by public reading, however, or merely writing papers on philanthropic subjects, the extreme usefulness of women has been demonstrated beyond dispute by the Social Science Association. It is no longer "an experiment to be tried," and we can hardly refrain from smiling at one critic's complacent assertion that it is "an innovation to be suppressed." (Parenthetically, we must express our curiosity to see the gentleman who will succeed in "suppressing" some of these ladies —Miss Carpenter, for instance—and in restoring them to crochet, potichomanie, and "diffidence.")

In nearly every department of the work there have been found ladies able and willing to afford substantial assistance; and, if it *were* true that some of them offered rather weak papers (or papers which sounded weak, being mangled in the reading by male substitutes), we venture to ask how many strong speeches are to be heard in *any* meeting, even such as are composed exclusively of gentlemen? In noting the progress of the Social Science Association, we trace everywhere the successful labours of women. While the public universally testify their sense of the excellent management of the congresses by the Founder and Secretary, Mr. Hastings, he himself publicly concedes no small share of the credit of his success to the aid of his assistant, the poetess, Miss Isa Craig, whose business talents excite the admiration of all connected with the Society. Lord Brougham announced, in 1859, that the most important papers hitherto presented had been those of Florence Nightingale, of which the Council thought it well to send copies to all the hospitals in the kingdom. It were idle to talk of the share which Mary Carpenter has had in one of the noblest departments of Social Science—the reformation of juvenile criminals, and the education of vagrants and paupers. While the venerable Recorder of Birmingham has been the soul of the great movement for the reform of criminals, his daughters have worthily followed in his steps, and done most excellent service by affording us accurate accounts of the more important foreign and colonial reformatory institutions. Each of the three affiliated societies is worked almost exclusively by women. Lord Shaftesbury said, in his opening address to the Association at Bradford, "Not a little is due to the share which women have taken, and most beneficially taken, in the business of this Society. I insist especially *on the value and peculiar nature of the assistance.* Men may do what must be done on a large scale; but, the instant the work becomes individual, and personal, the instant it requires tact and feeling, from that instant it passes into the hands of women. It is essentially their province, in which may be exercised all their moral powers, and all their intellectual faculties. It will give them their full share in the vast operations the world is yet to see."

Truly we believe it; and the Social Science Association will, we apprehend, reckon hereafter as not the least among its many achievements, that it has afforded the best and most appropriate of fields for the employment by women of one of the many powers disused by them hitherto, but doubtless designed by the Giver of every good gift to aid them to serve and bless mankind.

# ESSAY II.

## CELIBACY *v.* MARRIAGE.

*Reprinted from Fraser's Magazine, February,* 1862.

*How to be Happy though Married,* was the rather significant title of a quaint little treatise of the seventeenth century, still to be perused in old libraries. "Le mariage," says Fénelon, "est un état de tribulation très pénible auquel il faut se préparer en esprit de pénitence quand ons'y croit appelé." * Between these views of holy matrimony and those popularly attributed to Belgravian mothers, there exists so vast a difference that we cannot but suggest (considering the importance of the subject), that the Social Science Association should appoint a special department to examine the matter. Male and female reformers would find topics for many interesting papers in debating the relative benefits to society of "selfish domestic felicity," and sublimely "disinterested celibacy," as now inculcated from many quarters. An able article has lately appeared in a contemporary periodical, entitled "Keeping up Appearances." It

* Sentimens et Avis Chrétiens, chap. 1.

propounds, in brief, the following doctrine:—"That it is not a question of appearances, but of very substantial realities, whether a family in the rank of gentlefolk have to live on three or four hundred a year in England; that where this is the case it is impossible but that Paterfamilias, be he lawyer, doctor, divine, or man of letters, must needs, in all his ways and works, regard, *not* the pure aim of his profession, but the pecuniary interests involved therein. His wife is oppressed with household cares, and his children have hardly the means of health and suitable education. Under these circumstances, no man with common feelings can act with the same disregard of mercenary considerations as he might do were he living alone on an income sufficient to supply his bachelor necessities. He must needs "keep an eye to the main chance," and consider at all moments, how will it pay for me to act in this manner? Can I afford to offend this influential man, to write this outspoken book, to preach this unpopular doctrine? Thus we arrive at the very awkward conclusion that all the most gifted and devoted men who do not happen to inherit £1,000 a year, or to fall in love with an heiress, are bound in honour never to marry, at least until that goodly maturity of years when their professional earnings may have realized such an income. In a word, all our best men must be celibates—all our women who marry at all must put up with rather mercenary husbands (always excepting elder sons), and all the children of the next generation must be born of parents the least likely to convey to them any remarkable faculties or exalted principles. Ragnarok, of course, may be expected in the ensuing century.

Now this argument is much too cogent in itself, and much too well urged from really noble points of view, not to deserve serious investigation. If it be indeed true that no married man with small means can be perfectly disinterested, then we have come upon a new and most important item to be added to that sum of objections to wedlock, which the present order of things is daily bringing forward. As the expediency system of ethics is passing out of men's minds, the notion gains ground that all true work must be *disinterested* work. We begin dimly to perceive the truth that in human nature there are too great forces, one all noble and generous; the centrifugal force of LOVE, which carries us out of and above ourselves; the other, all base and narrow, the centripetal force of SELFISM, which brings us back to our own personal interests and desires. Every profession may be followed in one or other of these ways. Statescraft, war, science, art, philanthropy, may be pursued from pure love of our country or our kind, pure devotion to truth, or beauty, or justice. Or, on the other hand, they may be followed from selfish ambition, personal interest, and vanity. Our *affections* obey the same law, for we may love our friends for their own sakes, and be willing to give our happiness for theirs;

or we may love them merely for our selfish gratification in their intercourse, striving not to make them better and happier, but to narrow them heart and soul to ourselves. Our *moral* natures are in the same case, for we may obey the law of duty from simple allegiance to the eternal right, with the motto in our hearts, *Fais ce que doit advienne que pourra;* or we may be just, and true, and charitable, for the sake of human reward on earth or celestial payment in heaven. And, finally, even *religion* may be pure, or may be selfish. We may love God himself because He is supremely, infinitely good, and worthy of the love of all the hearts He has made; or we may serve Him with souls filled with servile fears and selfish hopes, favoured servants in a disfavoured universe, offering to the holy Lord of Good the homage which Ecloge and Actè paid to Nero.

Yes! If anything good, or noble, is ever to be done on earth, it must be done *disinterestedly.* The man of action and the man of thought must alike work because they love the true, the good, the beautiful, and genuinely desire (each in his own way) to realize them on earth. If their own interest cannot be wholly forgotten, yet it must be entirely subordinated to the nobler aim. The clergyman must preach what he finds to be true; the statesman legislate as he thinks right; the poet write what he feels to be beautiful; and none of them deign to consider—Will this sermon stop my preferment? Will this Act of Parliament offend my party? Will this book draw on me the lash of such a Review? He who truly achieves any good on earth, must surely do it in this spirit of disinterested devotion.

Now is it true that marriage without wealth must curb and check all these nobler impulses? Must the husband and father be a baser man, at all events a less true and brave one, than he was as a bachelor? If not selfish for himself, must he now grow wife-selfish, child-selfish, interested for those who belong to him, as he would disdain to be for himself?

It must be admitted this is a difficult question. There seems no small danger that the answer must be one which would land us in the monstrous conclusion that the condition which God has appointed as the natural one for human beings, is calculated inevitably to debase their purest aspirations. To find a less deplorable solution, let us go further back in our problem. What have we assumed a wife to be? A wholly passive medium of expenditure, like a conservatory or a pack of hounds?

The author of the article under debate admits with astonishing candour, that the *woman's* interest and happiness are necessarily sacrificed by the proper fulfilment of the man's destiny. He quotes Kingsley's aphorism with approbation—

Man must work and woman must weep.

Truly this conclusion, whereby no inconsiderable portion of the human race is consigned to the highly unprofitable occupation of "weeping," might have excited some doubts of the accuracy of the foregoing ratiocinations. It is not easy, we should suppose, for women generally to accept this matter of "weeping" as the proper end of their creation! At all events, if they occasionally indulge henceforth in the solace of tears, we cannot believe they will shed them for the loss of the connubial felicity to be enjoyed with those "workers," who so readily appoint them such a place in the order of the world.

Leaving aside, however, this piece of "muscular sociology," let us seriously inquire whether the true destiny of woman, if rightly understood, would not serve to make right this puzzle of life, and show that *if the wife were what the wife should be,* the husband would not need to grow more mercenary and more worldly to supply her wants, but would rather find her pure and religious influence raise him to higher modes of thinking, and a nobler and more devoted life, than either man or woman can attain alone.

The *actual* fact must, alas! be admitted. The cares of a family have a tendency to make a man interested; and what is much worse, the wife too frequently uses her influence the wrong way, and prompts her husband even to more worldly and prudential considerations than he would be inclined spontaneously to entertain.

Woman's natural refinement leads her to give too

high a value to outward polish, and, consequently, to tend always to seek social intercourse above her own natural circle. It is nearly always the *wives* of shopkeepers, merchants, professional men, and the smaller gentry, who are found pushing their families into the grade a step higher, and urging the often-recalcitrant husband to the needful toadyism and expenditure. Woman is Conservative, or rather feudal, by instinct, if she be not by some accident vehemently prejudiced the other way; and her unacknowledged but very real political influence is constantly exercised to check aspirations after progress of the rational kind

> Of Freedom slowly broadening down
> From precedent to precedent.

Worse than all, the education she now receives, makes her a bigot in religion. To *her*, the sources of wider and broader thought on the greatest of all subjects, are usually closed from childhood. The result is, that a timid and narrow creed constantly fetters the natural religious instincts of her heart, and she can exercise in no degree the influence over her husband's soul which her genuine piety might otherwise effect. If he venture to speak to her of the limits of his belief, she gives him reproach instead of sympathy; if he tell her he doubts the conclusions of her favourite preacher, she bursts into tears! Men have kept women from all share in the religious progress of the age, and the deplorable result is, that women are notoriously the drags on that progress. Instead of feeling like their Teuton forefathers, that their wives were "in nearer intercourse with the divinity than men," the Englishmen of to-day feel that their wives are the last persons with whom they can seek sympathy on religious matters. Half with tenderness for their good hearts, half with contempt for their weak minds, they leave them to the faith of the nursery, and seek for congenial intercourse only among men, hardheaded and honest, perhaps, in the fullest degree, yet without a woman's native spring of trust and reverence.

All these things tend to make wives fail in performing their proper part of inspiring feelings of devotion to noble causes. And further, a woman's ignorance of real life leads her to attach to outward show a value which it actually bears only in the opinion of other women as foolish as herself, and by no means in the eyes of anything which deserves to be called society at large. The *real* world—"the world of women and men,"

> Alive with sorrow and sin,
> Alive with pain and with passion,

does *not* concern itself so very earnestly with the number of the domestics and the antiquity of the millinery of its friends, as these ladies fondly imagine. Mrs. Grundy *lives*—she is a fact; but she is a very small and unimportant fact in life. Anybody with an ounce of pluck may cut Mrs. Grundy dead in the street, and never be troubled by her again. People do want some few things to make up their ideas of a gentleman or a lady, but they are not exactly what may be bought for even twice as many hundreds a year as our author has supposed, nor yet forfeited by the loss of any amount of stock in the Bank. A friend long resident in Italy, on reading these formidable statements, asked us ironically, "Pray, how many hundreds a year does it take to make a gentleman in England, and how many more go to making a lady?" No! we are not fallen so low as all this. Let a man or woman be honourable, refined, well-bred, agreeable in conversation: then there is little chance they will be turned out of the sphere to which they were born, because they keep two servants instead of a dozen, and use a hired cab instead of a carriage. It is miserable odious "flunkeyism" which attaches such infinite importance to these things; and the books of our day which represent them as holding the most prominent place in the thoughts of men, are utterly false to the realities of our social state. *Vanity Fair* is one stage of Pilgrim's Progress, but there are fifty others. To represent English social life as if it were the ineffable mass of meanness these books would make it, is a libel against human nature at which it is marvellous men do not rise in scorn and indignation.

"Ay—but," observed to us once a well-known writer, "all this meanness *is* a part of life! It is competent, then, to an author, if he please, to make it the staple of his fictions."

"And give them as true pictures of human nature?" we demanded.

"Yes, surely."

"We were in Egypt this year," we answered. "Suppose we gave an account of our *impressions de voyage*, and omitted all mention of the Nile, the Pyramids, the Sphynx, the palm-trees, and only described accurately certain small nocturnal troublers of our repose? Would that be a fair description of grand old Egypt? You know it would be quite *true?* There *were* those Becky Sharps!"

It is needless to discuss at any length how a wife's belief that these outward "appearances" are of real importance, must unfit her for properly meeting the problems of a limited income. She thinks it a good investment to expend on show, what would suffice to procure very substantial comforts. There *is* a great truth in the *Times*' observation—"All the meaner and more miserable part of economical cares and discussions refers to 'appearances;' for the sense of pettiness and shame cannot attach to the actual needs of health and comfort, but only to the aspect our poverty may bear in the eyes of those whom we are senseless enough to wish should suppose us to be rich." In particular, the wives of poor gentlemen seem almost invariably to make it a point of conscience to dress with more richness and variety than those of wealthy men. Delicate taste and a generally ladylike appearance will not suffice,—they must *prove* they are not poor, precisely because all their acquaintances know that they are so. Moire antique is the invariable uniform of the wives of unsuccessful physicians, briefless barristers, and younger sons.

But supposing these mistakes of women removed; suppose (what ought to be the ordinary course of the marriages of professional men) that the wife brings a portion which covers her added share of the joint household, and that she expends the common income judiciously. Here is the material basis for a well-ordered life. Now, does it appear that the husband in such a case is likely to be less disinterested than he was when he was single? There is only one answer. It depends on the wife's own character. If she encourage him in every noble aim and disinterested action, it will hardly happen but that he will keep up to his former standard—nay, rise far above it. On the other hand, if she urge selfish considerations at every turn; if she palliate meanness and deprecate self-sacrifice;—then indeed the natural temptations of avarice and selfish ambition *have* a most powerful, almost an invincible ally in the wife, faithless to her holy duty of sustaining her husband's soul in life's great battle.

It is little understood how in all human relations the moral influences we begin by exercising, go on re-acting *ad infinitum* from one to the other in proportion to the closeness of the relationship. A (we will suppose) starts, by a little weak fondness, encouraging B to some small piece of selfishness or indolence, because he is fatigued. B cannot well help returning the compliment shortly, and making excuses for A not performing some duty on account of the weather. Next day it is an unkind sentiment, which passes unchecked; then a harsh word; and so on and so on. On the other hand, if, with whatever effort, the one encourage the other to exert himself—to sacrifice comfort for duty—to think kindly of disagreeable people—to speak only what is right and sincere,—then from that side also comes an influence raising step by step the virtue of the other. In higher ways still, the same truth holds good. Any two people who live much together (even in less tender connexion than husband and wife), cannot fail most importantly to colour each other's views of the great purposes of life. Live with one to whom the centripetal force of Selfism is paramount, and it is hardly possible to avoid contemplating everything from a selfish point of view. Live with one for ever carried beyond his own interests by the centrifugal force of pure Love for truth, for right, for man, for God, and it is impossible but that the divine fire in such a breast will kindle the embers in our own, till we blush to remember we have lived for lower aims and our own poor paltry hap piness.

These discussions on the moral aspects of marriage

assume a special significance at this moment, since from many other quarters obstacles are arising which must all tend towards rendering (for a long time, at least) celibacy more and more common and desirable. We have heard, perhaps, more than enough of these obstacles on the *man's* side. Let us, therefore, turn for a moment to consider those which must render women less willing than formerly to enter into such relation.

In the first place, till lately the condition of an unmarried woman of the upper classes was so shackled by social prejudices that it was inevitably a dreary and monotonous one. Mostly, the "old maid" lived in a small house or lodging, out of which she rarely dared to sally on any journey, and where, with a few female friends as closely limited as herself, she divided her life, as the Frenchman has it, between "*la médisance, le jeu, et la dévotion.*" A society of these unhappy ones was once not inappropriately nicknamed by a witty nobleman "the Bottled Wasps." It is half piteous, half ridiculous, to hear of the trifles which occupy these poor shrivelled hearts and minds. We once called on a very worthy and even clever member of the sisterhood residing in Bath. Her features were discomposed—her voice somewhat shriller than usual. We inquired considerately of the cause of affliction.

"I am going to leave my lodgings."

"I am sorry to hear it. They seem very nice."

"Yes, yes; but I can bear it no longer! Do you

not observe there are two mats in the passage—one at the hall-door, one at the door of my room?"

"It escaped my notice."

"Well, there they are. And for seven-and-twenty times—I have counted them!—seven-and-twenty times the people of the house have passed by the mat at the hall door and come and wiped their feet on my mat, and made me think visitors were coming, and get off the sofa and take off my spectacles; and then nobody came in! I am going away to-morrow."

I think, however, this sort of existence will probably end with the present generation. The "old maid" of 1861 is an exceedingly cheery personage, running about untrammelled by husband or children; now visiting her relatives' country houses, now taking her month in town, now off to a favourite *pension* on Lake Geneva, now scaling Vesuvius or the Pyramids. And, what is better, she has found not only freedom of locomotion, but a sphere of action peculiarly congenial to her nature. "My life, and what shall I do with it?" is a problem for which she finds the happiest solution ready to her hand in schools and hospitals without number. No longer does the Church of Rome monopolize the truth, that on a woman who has no husband, parent, or child, *every* sick and suffering man, every aged childless woman, every desolate orphan, has a claim. She has not fewer duties than other women, only more diffused ones. The "old maid's" life may be as rich, as blessed, as that of the proudest of mothers with her crown of clustering babes. Nay, she feels that in the power of devoting her *whole* time and energies to some benevolent task, she is enabled to effect perhaps some greater good than would otherwise have been possible. "On n'enfante les grandes œuvres que dans la virginité."

And further, if a woman have but strength to make up her mind to a single life, she is enabled by nature to be far more independently happy therein than a man in the same position. A man, be he rich or poor, who returns at night to a home adorned by no woman's presence and domestic cares, is at best dreary and uncomfortable. But a woman makes her home for herself, and surrounds herself with the atmosphere of taste and the little details of housewifely comforts. If she have no sister, she has yet inherited the blessed power of a woman to make true and tender friendships, such as not one man's heart in a hundred can even imagine; and while he smiles scornfully at the idea of friendship meaning anything beyond acquaintance at a club, or the intimacy of a barrack, she enjoys one of the purest of pleasures and the most unselfish of all affections.

Nor does the "old maid" contemplate a solitary age as the bachelor must usually do. It will go hard but she will find a *woman* ready to share it. And more! —(but it is a theme we may not treat of here). She thinks to *die*, if without having given or shared some of the highest joys of human nature, yet at least without having caused one fellow-being to regret she was born to tempt to sin and shame. We ask it in all solemn sadness—Do the *men* who resolve on an unmarried life, fixedly purpose also so to die with as spotless a conscience ?

And on the other hand, while the utility, freedom, and happiness of a single woman's life have become greater, the *knowledge* of the risks of an unhappy marriage (if not the risks themselves) has become more public. The Divorce Court, in righting the most appalling wrongs to which the members of a civilized community could be subjected, has revealed secrets which must tend to modify immensely our ideas of English domestic felicity. Well it is that these hideous revelations should take place, for, as Carlyle says, "To nothing but error can any truth be dangerous;" and the fatal error of hasty marriage is constantly due to ignorance of the possibilities of some forms of offence among the apparently respectable classes of society. It has always been vaguely known, indeed, that both husbands and wives sometimes broke their most solemn vows and fell into sin; but it was reserved for the new law to show how many hundreds of such tragedies underlie the outwardly decorous lives, not only of the long-blamed aristocracy, but of the middle ranks in England. But beside that most grievous wrong, who imagined that the wives of English *gentlemen* might be called on to endure from their husbands the violence and cruelty we are accustomed to picture exercised only in the lowest lanes and courts of our cities, where drunken ruffians, stumbling home from the gin-palace, assail the miserable partners of their vices with curses, kicks, and blows? Who could have imagined it possible, that well-born and well-educated men, in honourable professions, should be guilty of the same brutality? Imagine a handsomely-furnished drawing-room, with its books, and flowers, and lights, and all the refinements of civilized life, for the scene of similar outrages. Imagine the offender a well-dressed gentleman, tall and powerful as English gentlemen are wont to be; the victim shrinking from his blows—a gentle, high-bred English *lady!* Good God! does not the picture make every true man set his teeth, and clench his hand?

Now these things *are* so. The Divorce Court has brought dozens of them to light; and we all know well that for one wife who will seek public redress for her wrongs, there are always ten, who, for their childrens' sakes, will bear their martyrdoms in silence. True martyrs they are—the sorest tried, perhaps, of any in the world—God help and comfort them! But single women can surely hardly forget these things, or fail to hesitate to try a lottery in which there may be one chance in a thousand of such a destiny. Thus, then, on the man's side, we have got arrayed against marriage all the arguments we have heard so often—economy, independence, freedom of risk of an uncongenial, a bad-tempered, a sickly, or an unfaithful wife;

and, lastly, this new principle, that, to pursue his calling disinterestedly, he must be untrammelled by the ties of a dependent family. And, on the woman's side, we have got a no less formidable range of objections; the certainty now offered to her of being able to make for herself a free, useful, and happy life alone, and the demonstrated danger of being inexpressibly miserable should she choose either an unfaithful or a cruel husband.

The conclusion seems inevitable, that marriage will become more and more rare, in spite of all Belgravian or other mothers can do. Instead of all young men intending, at some time or other, to marry, and all young women looking forward to be wives, we shall find many of them both resolving on a celibate life.

But the tide must turn at last. Marriage was manifestly the Creator's plan for humanity, and therefore we cannot doubt that it will eventually become the rule of all men and women's lives. When that time arrives, both sexes will have learned weighty lessons. The Englishman of the twentieth century will abandon those claims of marital authority, whose residue he still inherits from days when might made right, and from lands of Eastern sensuality, where woman is first the slave of her own weakness, and then inevitably the slave of man. When the theory of the "Divine Right of Husbands" has followed to limbo that of the "Divine Right of Kings," and a precedency in selfishness is no longer assumed to be the sacred privilege of masculine strength and wisdom, then will become possible a conjugal love and union nobler and more tender by far than can ever exist while such claims are even tacitly supposed. Of all true, holy, human love, as distinguished from the love of the hound and the slave, Chaucer said right well—

> When mastery cometh, then sweet Love anon
> Flappeth his nimble wings, and soon away is gone.

And abandoning his authority (save such as real wisdom and power of nature must ever secure), man will also abandon that direful licence of which we hear so much—the licence to be less pure and faithful than a woman while escaping the same penalty of disgrace. Then will the husband bring to his wife feelings as fresh as those which now are too often her contribution alone to their joint happiness.

And the Englishwoman of the twentieth century will, on her part, learn to rise above her present pitiful ambitions of social advancement and petty personal vanity—the thousand childish foibles in which she now thinks it her right to indulge. She will be ready to cope with poverty, and encourage her husband cheerfully to bear it for life, rather than sully the noblest of his aspirations. She will learn that no longer must morality be divided between them; Truth and Courage for him, and Chastity and Patience for her; but that she, too, must be true as an honourable *man* is true, and brave in her own sphere of duty as he is brave in his, if she would exchange his half-contemptuous gallantry for genuine respect. And, finally, she will share her husband's religion, she will boldly confront the doubts of his understanding by the intuitions of her heart; she will help him to *love*, as he will help her to *knowledge*. And thus together may they reach a nobler and a warmer faith than the world yet has seen.

# ESSAY III.

## WHAT SHALL WE DO WITH OUR OLD MAIDS?

*Reprinted from Fraser's Magazine for November*, 1862.

IN the Convocation of Canterbury for this year of 1862, the readers of such journals as report in full the sayings and doings of that not very interesting assembly, were surprised to find the subject of Protestant Sisterhoods, or Deaconesses, discussed with an unanimity of feeling almost unique in the annals of ecclesiastic parliaments. High Churchmen and Low, Broad Churchmen and Hard, all seemed agreed that there was good work for women to do, and which women *were* doing all over England; and that it was extremely desirable that all these lady guerillas of philanthropy should be enrolled in the regular disciplined army of the Church, together with as many new recruits as might be enlisted. To use a more appropriate simile, Mother Church expressed herself satisfied at her daughters "coming out," but considered that her chaperonage was decidedly necessary to their decorum.

Again, at the Social Science Congress of this summer, in London, the employment of women, the education of women, and all the other rights and wrongs of women, were urged, if not with a unanimity equal to that of their reverend predecessors, yet with, at the very least, equal animation. It is quite evident that the subject is not to be allowed to go to sleep, and we may as well face it valiantly, and endeavour to see light through its complications, rather than attempt to lecture the female sex generally on the merits of a "golden silence," and the propriety of adorning themselves with that decoration (doubtless modestly declined, as too precious for their own use, by masculine reviewers), "the ornament of a meek and quiet spirit." In a former article ("Celibacy *v.* Marriage," *Fraser's Magazine* for April, 1862) we treated the subject in part. We now propose to pursue it further, and investigate in particular the new phases which it has lately assumed.

The questions involved may be stated very simply.

It appears that there is a natural excess of four or five per cent. of females over the males in our population. This, then, might be assumed to be the limits within which female celibacy was normal and inevitable.

There is, however, an actual ratio of thirty per cent of women now in England who never marry, leaving one-fourth of both sexes in a state of celibacy. This proportion further appears to be constantly on the increase. It is obvious enough that these facts call for a revision of many of our social arrangements. The old assumption that marriage was the sole destiny of woman, and that it was the business of her husband to afford her support, is brought up short by the statement that one woman in four is certain not to marry, and that three millions of women earn their own living at this moment in England. We may view the case two ways: either—

1st. We must frankly accept this new state of things, and educate women and modify trade in accordance therewith, so as to make the condition of celibacy as little injurious as possible; or,—

2nd. We must set ourselves vigorously to stop the current which is leading men and women away from the natural order of Providence. We must do nothing whatever to render celibacy easy or attractive; and we must make the utmost efforts to promote marriage by emigration of women to the colonies, and all other means in our power.

The second of these views we shall in the first place consider. It may be found to colour the ideas of a vast number of writers, and to influence essentially the decisions made on many points—as the admission of women to university degrees, to the medical profession, and generally to free competition in employment. Lately it has met a powerful and not unkindly exposition in an article in a contemporary quarterly, entitled, "Why are Women Redundant?" Therein it is plainly set forth that all efforts to make celibacy easy for women are labours in a wrong direction, and are to be likened to the noxious exertions of quacks to mitigate the symptoms of disease, and allow the patient to persist in his evil courses. The root of the malady should be struck at, and marriage, the only true vocation for women, promoted at any cost, even by the most enormous schemes for the deportation of 440,000 females. Thus alone (and by the enforcing of a stricter morality on men) should the evil be touched. As to making the labours of single women remunerative, and their lives free and happy, all such mistaken philanthropy will but tend to place them in a position more and more false and unnatural. Marriage will then become to them a matter of "cold philosophic choice," and accordingly may be expected to be more and more frequently declined.

There is a great deal in this view of the case which, on the first blush, approves itself to our minds, and we have not been surprised to find the article in question quoted as of the soundest common sense. All, save ascetics and visionaries, must admit that, for the mass of mankind, marriage is the right condition, the happiest, and the most conducive to virtue. This position fairly and fully conceded, it *might* appear that the whole of the consequences deduced followed of necessity, and that the direct promotion of marriage and discountenancing of celibacy was all we had to do in the matter.

A little deeper reflection, however, discloses a very important point which has been dropped out of the argument. Marriage is, indeed, the happiest and best condition for mankind. But does any one think that all marriages are so? When we make the assertion that marriage is good and virtuous, do we mean a marriage of interest, a marriage for wealth, for position, for rank, for support? Surely nothing of the kind. Such marriages as these are the sources of misery and sin, not of happiness and virtue; nay, their moral character, to be fitly designated, would require stronger words than we care to use. There is only one kind of marriage which makes good the assertion that it is the right and happy condition for mankind, and that is a marriage founded on free choice, esteem, and affection—in one word, on love. If, then, we seek to promote the happiness and virtue of the community, our efforts must be directed to encouraging *only* marriages which are of the sort to produce them—namely, marriages founded on love. All marriages founded on interest, on the desire for position, support, or the like, we must discourage to the utmost of our power, as the sources of nothing but wretchedness. Where, now, have we reached? Is it not to the conclusion that to make it a woman's *interest* to marry, to force her, by barring out every means of self-support and all fairly remunerative labour, to look to marriage as her sole chance of competency, is precisely to drive her into one of those sinful and unhappy marriages? It is quite clear we can never drive her into *love.* That is a sentiment which poverty, friendlessness, and helplessness can by no means call out. Nor, on the contrary, can competence and freedom in any way check it. It will arise under its natural conditions, if we will but leave the matter alone. A *loving* marriage can never become a matter of "cold philosophic choice." And if *not* a loving one, then, for heaven's sake, let us give no motive for choice at all.

Let the employments of women be raised and multiplied as much as possible, let their labour be as fairly remunerated, let their education be pushed as high, let their whole position be made as healthy and happy as possible, and there will come out once more, here as in every other department of life, the triumph of the Divine laws of our nature. Loving marriages are (we cannot doubt) what God has designed, not marriages of interest. When we have made it less women's interest to marry, we shall indeed have less and fewer interested marriages, with all their train of miseries and evils. But we shall also have more *loving* ones, more marriages founded on free choice and free affection. Thus we arrive at the conclusion that for the very end of promoting marriage—that is, such marriage as it is alone desirable to promote—we should pursue a precisely opposite course to that suggested by the reviewer or his party. Instead of leaving single women as helpless as possible, and their labour as ill-rewarded—instead of dinning into their ears from childhood that marriage is their one vocation and concern in life, and securing afterwards if they miss it that they shall find no other vocation or concern;—instead of all this, we shall act exactly on the reverse principle. We shall make single life so free and happy that they shall have not one temptation to change it save the only temptation which *ought* to determine them—namely, love. Instead of making marriage a case of "Hobson's choice" for a woman, we shall endeavour to give her such independence of all interested considerations that she may make it a choice, not indeed "cold and philosophic," but warm from the heart, and guided by heart and conscience only.

And again, in another way the same principle holds good, and marriage will be found to be best promoted by aiding and not by thwarting the efforts of single women to improve their condition. It is a topic on which we cannot speak much, but thus far may suffice. The reviewer alludes with painful truth to a class of the community whose lot is far more grievous than either celibacy or marriage. Justly he traces the unwillingness of hundreds of men to marry to the existence of these unhappy women in their present condition. He would remedy the evil by preaching marriage to such men. But does not all the world know that thousands of these poor souls of all degrees would never have fallen into their miserable vocation had any *other* course been open to them, and they had been enabled to acquire a competence by honest labour? Let such honest courses be opened to them, and then we shall see, as in America, the recruiting of that wretched army becoming less and less possible every year in the country. The self-supporting, and therefore self-respecting woman may indeed become a wife, and a good and happy one, but she will no longer afford any man a reason for declining to marry.

It is curious to note that while, on the one hand, we are urged to make marriage the sole vocation of women, we are simultaneously met on the other by the outpourings of ridicule and contempt on all who for themselves, or even for their children, seek ever so indirectly to attain this vocation. Only last year all England was entertained by jests concerning "Belgravian mothers;" and the wiles and devices of widows and damsels afford an unending topic of satire and amusement in private and public. Now we ask, in all seriousness, Wherefore all this ridicule and contempt? *If* marriage be indeed the one object of a woman's life—*if* to give her any other pursuit or interest be only to divert her from that one object and "palliate the symptoms while fostering a great social disease"—then, we repeat, *why* despise these match-making mothers? Are they to do nothing to help their daughters to their only true vocation, which, if they should miss, their lives *ought* to be failures, poverty-stricken and miserable? Nay; but if things be so, the most open, unblushing marketing of their daughters is the *duty* of parents, and the father or mother who leaves the matter to chance is flagrantly neglectful. Truly it is a paradox passing all limits of reason, that society should enforce marriage on woman as her only honourable life, and at the same time should stigmatize as dishonourable the efforts of her parents to settle her in marriage.

The spontaneous sentiment of mankind has hit a deeper truth than the theories of economists. It *is* in the nature of things disgraceful and abominable that marriage should be made the aim of a woman's life. It can only become what it is meant to be, the completion and crown of the life of either man or woman, when it has arisen from sentiments which can never be bespoken for the convenient fulfilment of any vocation whatsoever.

But it is urged, and not unreasonably—If it be admitted on all hands that marriage is the best condition, and that only one-fourth of the female sex do not marry, how can we expect provision to be made for this contingency of one chance in four by a girl's parents and by herself, in going through an education (perhaps costly and laborious) for a trade or profession which there are three chances in four she will not long continue to exercise?

It must be admitted here is the great knot and

difficulty of the higher branches of woman's employment. It does require far-seeing care on the part of the parent, perseverance and resolution of no mean order on that of the daughter, to go through in youth the training which will fit her to earn her livelihood hereafter in any of the more elevated occupations. Nay, it demands that she devote to such training the precise years of life wherein the chances of marriage are commonly offered, and the difficulties of pursuing a steady course are very much enhanced by temptations of all kinds. If she wait till the years when such chances fail, and take up a pursuit at thirty, merely as a *pis aller*, she must inevitably remain for ever behindhand and in an inferior position.

The trial is undoubtedly considerable; but there are symptoms that both young women and their parents will not be always unwilling to meet it, and to invest both time and money in lines of education which may, indeed, prove superfluous, but which likewise may afford the mainstay of a life which, without them, would be helpless, aimless, and miserable. The magnitude of the risk ought surely to weigh somewhat in the balance. At the lowest point of view, a woman is no worse off if she marry eventually, for having first gone through an education for some good pursuit; while, if she remain single, she is wretchedly off for not having had such education. But this is, in fact, only a half-view of the case. As we have insisted before, it is only on the standing-ground of a happy and independent celibacy that a woman can really make a free choice in marriage. To secure this standing-ground, a pursuit is more needful than a pecuniary competence, for a life without aim or object is one which, more than all others, goads a woman into accepting any chance of a change. Mariana (we are privately convinced) would have eloped out of the Moated Grange not only with that particular "he" who never came, but with any other suitor who might have presented himself! Only a woman who has something else than making love to do and to think of, will love really and deeply. It is in *real lives*—lives devoted to actual service of father or mother, or to work of some kind for God or man—that alone spring up *real feelings.* Lives of idleness and pleasure have no depth to nourish such plants.

Again, we are very far indeed from maintaining that *during* marriage it is at all to be desired that a woman should struggle to keep up whatever pursuit she had adopted beforehand. In nine cases out of ten this will drop naturally to the ground, especially when she has children. The great and paramount duties of a mother and wife once adopted, every other interest sinks, by the beneficent laws of our nature, into a subordinate place in normally constituted minds, and the effort to perpetuate them is as false as it is usually fruitless. Where necessity and poverty compel mothers in the lower ranks to go out to work, we all know too well the evils which ensue. And in the higher classes doubtless the holding tenaciously by any pursuit interfering with home duties must produce such Mrs. Jellabys as we sometimes hear of. It is not only leisure which is in question. There appear to be some occult laws in woman's nature providing against such mistakes by rendering it impossible to pursue the higher branches of art or literature, or any work tasking mental exertion, while home and motherly cares have their claims. We have heard of a great artist saying that she is always obliged to leave her children for a few weeks before she can throw herself again into the artist-feeling of her youth, and we believe her experience is corroborated on all hands. No great books have been written, or works achieved by women while their children were around them in infancy. No woman can lead the two lives at the same time.

But it is often strangely forgotten that there are such things as Widows, left such in the prime of life, and quite as much needing occupation as if they had remained single. Another chance must fairly be added to our one in four that a woman may need such a pursuit as we have supposed. She may never marry, or, having married, she may be left a childless widow, or a widow whose few children occupy but a portion of her time. Suppose, for instance, she has been a physician. How often would the possibility of returning to her early profession be an invaluable resource after her husband's death! The greatest female mathematician living was saved from despairing sorrow in widowhood, by throwing herself afresh into the studies of her youth.

It may be a pleasantly romantic idea to some minds, that of woman growing up solely with the hope of becoming some man's devoted wife, marrying the first that offers, and, when he dies, becoming a sort of moral Suttee whose heart is supposed to be henceforth dead and in ashes. But it is quite clear that Providence can never have designed any such order of things. All the infinite tenderness and devotion He has placed in women's hearts, though meant to make marriage blessed and happy, and diffusing as from a hearth of warm affections, kindness and love on all around, is yet meant to be subordinated to the great purposes of the existence of all rational souls—the approximation to God through virtue. With reverence be it spoken, GOD is the only true centre of life for us all; not any creature He has made. "To live unto God" is the law for man and woman alike. Whoever strives to do this will neither spend youth in longing for happiness which may be withheld, nor age in despair for that which may be withdrawn.

To resume. It appears that from every point of view in which we regard the subject, it is desirable that women should have other aims, pursuits, and interests in life beside matrimony, and that by possessing them they are guaranteed against being driven into unloving marriages, and rendered more fitted for loving ones, while their single life, whether in maidenhood or widowhood, is made useful and happy.

Before closing this part of the subject, we cannot but add a few words to express our amused surprise at the way in which the writers on this subject constantly concern themselves with the question of *female* celibacy, deplore it, abuse it, propose amazing remedies for it, but take little or no notice of the twenty-five per cent. old bachelors (or thereabouts), who needs must exist to match the thirty per cent. old maids. *Their* moral condition seems to excite no alarm, their lonely old age no foreboding compassion, their action on the community no reprobation. Nobody scolds them very seriously, unless some stray Belgravian grandmother. All the alarm, compassion, reprobation, and scoldings are reserved for the poor old maids. But of the two, which of the parties is the chief delinquent? The *Zend Avesta*, as translated by Anquetil du Perron, contains somewhere this awful denunciation:—"That damsel who, having reached the age of eighteen, shall refuse to marry, must remain in hell till the Resurrection!" A severe penalty, doubtless, for the crime, and wonderful to meet in the mild creed of Zoroaster, where no greater punishment is allotted to any offence whatsoever. Were these Guebre young ladies so terribly cruel, and *mazdiesnans* (true believers) so desperately enamoured? Are we to imagine the obdurate damsels despatching whole dozens of despairing gentlemen in conical caps to join the society in the shades below—

> Hapless youths who died for love,
> Wandering in a myrtle grove!

It takes a vivid stretch of imagination in England, in the nineteenth century, to picture anything of the kind. Whatever other offences our young ladies may be guilty of, or other weaknesses our young gentlemen, obduracy on the one hand, and dying for love on the other, are rarities, at all events. Yet one would suppose that Zoroaster was needed over here, to judge of the manner in which old maids are lectured on their very improper position. "The Repression of Crime," as the benevolent Recorder of Birmingham would phrase it, seems on the point of being exercised against them, since it has been found out that their offence is on the increase, like poaching in country districts and landlord shooting in Ireland. The mildest punishment, we are told, is to be transportation, to which half a million have just been condemned, and for the terror of future evil doers, it is decreed that no single woman's work ought to be fairly remunerated, nor her position allowed to be entirely respectable, lest she exercise "a cold philosophic choice" about matrimony. No false charity to criminals! Transportation or starvation to all old maids!

Poor old maids! Will not the Reformatory Union, or some other friends of the criminal, take their case in hand? They are too old for Miss Carpenter.

Could not Sir Walter Crofton's Intermediate System be of some use? There is reason to hope that many of them would be willing to adopt a more honest way of life were the chance offered them.

If the reader should have gone with us thus far, we shall be able better to follow the subject from a point of view which shall in fact unite the two leading ideas of which we made mention at starting. We shall, with the *first*, seek earnestly how the condition of single women may be most effectually improved; and with the *second*, we shall admit the promotion of marriage (*provided it be disinterested and loving*) to be the best end to which such improvements will tend.

In one point there is a practical unanimity between the schemes of the two parties, and this we should desire to notice before proceeding to consider the ways in which the condition of single women may be improved as such. The scheme is that of emigration for women to the colonies. Here we have multitudes of women offered in the first place remunerative employment beyond anything they could obtain at home; and further, the facilitation of marriage effected for large numbers, to the great benefit of both men and women. What there might appear in the plan contradictory to the principles we have laid down above, is only apparent, and not real. The woman who arrives in a colony where her labour, of head or hands, can command an ample maintenance, stands in the precise condition we have desired to make marriage—

a matter of free choice. She has left "Hobson's choice" behind her with the poverty of England, and has come out to find competence and freedom, and if she choose (but *only* if she choose), marriage also.

It is needless to say that this scheme has our entire sympathy and good wishes, though we do not expect to live to see the time when our reviewer's plans will be fulfilled by the deportation of women at the rate of thirty or forty thousand a year.*

An important point, however, must not be overlooked. However far the emigration of women of the working classes may be carried, that of educated women must at all times remain very limited, inasmuch as the demand for them in the colonies is comparatively trifling. Now, it is of educated women that the great body of "old maids" consists; in the lower orders celibacy is rare. Thus, it should be borne in mind that emigration schemes do not essentially bear on the main point, "How shall we improve the condition of the thirty per cent. of single women in England?" The reviewer to whom we have so often alluded, does indeed dispose of the matter by observing that the transportation he fondly hopes to see effected, of 440,000 women to the colonies, will at

* We rejoice to hear that Miss Maria S. Rye, who has already done so much for this cause, is on the point of sailing to Otago with one hundred female emigrants, to superintend personally the arrangements for their welfare. This is doing woman's work in working style truly. [Miss Rye has carried out her intention, and is now at Otago. March, 1863.]

least *relieve the market* for those who remain. We cannot but fear, however, that the governesses and other ladies so accommodated will not much profit by the large selection thus afforded them among the blacksmiths and ploughmen, deprived of their proper companions. At the least we shall have a quarter of a million of old maids *in esse* and *in posse* left on hand. What can we do for them?

For convenience, we may divide them into two classes. One of them, without capital or high cultivation, needs employment suitable to a woman's powers, and yet affording better remuneration than woman's work has hitherto usually received. Here we find the efforts of Miss Faithfull, Miss Parkes, Miss Crowe, Miss Rye, and the other ladies in combination with the society founded by Miss Boucherett, labouring to procure such employment for them by the Victoria Printing Press, the Law Copying Office, and other plans in action or contemplated for watchmaking, hair-dressing, and the like. We may look on this class as in good hands; and as the emigration of women will actually touch it and carry away numbers of its members, we may hope that its destinies are likely henceforth to improve.

The other and higher class is that of which we desire more particularly to speak, namely, of ladies either possessed of sufficient pecuniary means to support themselves comfortably, or else of such gifts and cultivation as shall command a competence. The help these women need is not of a pecuniary nature, but a large portion of them require aid, and the removal of existing restrictions, to afford them the full exercise of their natural powers, and make their lives as useful and happy as Providence has intended. Of *all* the position is at the present moment of transition worthy of some attention, and suggestive of some curious speculations regarding the future of women. Channing remarks that when the negro races become thoroughly Christianized we shall see a development of the religion never known before. At least equally justly may we predict that when woman's gifts are at last expanded in an atmosphere of freedom and happiness, we shall find graces and powers revealed to us of which we yet have little dreamed. To the consideration, then, of the condition and prospects of women of the upper classes who remain unmarried, we shall devote the following pages.

All the pursuits of mankind, beside mere money-getting, may be fitly classed in three great orders. They are in one way or another the pursuit of the True, the Beautiful, or the Good. In a general way we may say that science, literature, and philosophy are devoted to Truth; art in all its branches (including poetic literature) to the Beautiful; and politics and philanthropy to the Good. Within certain limits, each of these lines of action are open to women; and it is in the aspect they bear as regards women's work that we are now to regard them. But before analysing them further, I would fain be allowed to make one remark which is far too often forgotten. Each of these pursuits is equally noble in itself; it is our fitness for one or the other, not its intrinsic sanctity or value, which ought to determine our choice; and we are all astray in our judgments if we come to the examination of them with prejudices for or against one or the other. In these days, when "the icy chains of custom and of prejudice" are somewhat loosened, and men and women go forth more freely than ever of old to choose and make their lives, there is too often this false measurement of our brother's choice. Each of us asks his friend in effect, if not in words—"Why not follow my calling rather than your own? Why not use such a gift? Why not adopt such a task?" The answer to these questions must not be made with the senseless pedantry of the assumption, that because to *us* art or literature, or philanthropy or politics, is the true vocation, therefore for all men and women it is the noblest; and that God meant Mozart to be a statesman, and Howard a sculptor, and Kant a teacher in a ragged school. The true, the beautiful, and the good are all revelations of the Infinite One, and therefore all holy. It is enough for a man if it be given him in his lifetime to pursue any one of them to profit—to carry a single step further the torch of humanity along either of the three roads, every one of which leads up to God. The philosopher, who studies and teaches us the laws of mind or matter—the artist, who beholds with illumined eyes the beauty of the world, and creates it afresh in poetry or painting—the statesman or philanthropist, who labours to make Right victorious, and to advance the virtue and happiness of mankind,—all these in their several ways are God's seers, God's prophets, as much the one as the other. We could afford to lose none of them, to undervalue none of them. The philosopher is not to be honoured only for the goodness or the beauty of the *truth* he has revealed. All truth is good and beautiful, but it is to be prized because it is *truth,* and not merely for its goodness or beauty. The artist is not to be honoured only for the truth or the goodness of the *beautiful* he has revealed. The beautiful is necessarily good and true, but it is to be loved because it is *beautiful,* and not merely for its truth or goodness.* Like the old Athanasian symbol, we may say, "The Truth is divine, the Beautiful is divine, and the Good is divine. And yet they are not three divine things, but three revelations of the One Divine Lord." If men would but feel this each in his own pursuit, and in judging of the pursuits of others, how holy and noble would all faithful work become! We are haunted yet with the Romish thought that a life of asceticism, of preaching, of prayer, of charity, is altogether on a different plane of being from a life devoted to other tasks. But it is not so. From *every* field of

* See Victor Cousin, "*Du Vrai, du Beau, et du Bien.*"

honest human toil there rises a ladder up into heaven. Was Kepler further from God than any Howard or Xavier when, after discovering the law of the planetary distances, he bowed his head and exclaimed in rapture, "O God, I think Thy thoughts after Thee!" Was Milton less divine than any St. Theresa locked in her stony cell, when his mighty genius had soared "upon the seraph wings of ecstasy" over the whole beautiful creation, and he poured out at last his triumphant Psalm—

> These are Thy glorious works, Parent of Good—
> Almighty!

Of these three great modes of Divine manifestation, it would appear, however, that, though equal in sanctity and dignity, the pursuit of the True and of the Beautiful were designed for comparatively few among mankind. Few possess the pure abstract love of Truth in such fervour as to fit them to become the martyrs of science or the prophets of philosophy. Few also are those who are endowed with that supreme sense of the Beautiful, and power to reproduce it in form, colour, or sound, which constitute the gifts of the artist. Especially does this hold good with women. While few of them do not feel their hearts warmed with the love of goodness, and the desire to relieve the sufferings of their fellows, a mere fraction, in comparison, interest themselves to any extent in the pursuit of the abstract truths of philosophy or science, or possess any powers to reproduce the Beautiful in Art, even when they have a perception of its presence in nature. We may discuss briefly, then, here the prospects of the employment of women in the departments of Truth and Beauty, and in a future paper consider more at length the new aspect of their philanthropic labours and endeavours to do Good.

Till of very late years it was, we think, perfectly justifiable to doubt the possibility of women possessing any creative artistic power. Receptive faculties they have always had, ready and vivid perception of the beautiful in both nature and art, delicate discrimination and refined taste, nay, the power (especially in music and the drama) of reproducing what the genius of man had created. But to originate any work of even second-rate merit was what no woman had done. Sappho was a mere name, and between her and even such a feeble poetess as Mrs. Hemans, there was hardly another to fill up the gap of the whole cycle of history. No woman has written the epics, nor the dramas, nay, nor even the national songs of her country, if we may not except Miriam's and Deborah's chants of victory. In music, nothing. In architecture, nothing. In sculpture, nothing. In painting, an Elisabetta Sirani, a Rosalba, an Angelica Kauffman —hardly exceptions enough to prove the rule. Such works as women did accomplish were all stamped with the same impress of feebleness and prettiness. As Mrs. Hemans and Joanna Baillie and Mrs. Tighe wrote poetry, so Angelica Kauffman painted pictures, and other ladies composed washy music and Minerva-press romances. If Tennyson's hero had spoken of woman's *Art* instead of woman's passions, he would have been as right for the one as he was wrong as regards the other. It *was*

> As moonlight is to sunlight
> And as water is to wine.

To coin an epithet from a good type of the school—it was all "Angelical," no flesh and blood at all, but super-refined sentiments and super-elongated limbs.

But there seem symptoms extant that this state of things is to undergo a change, and the works of women become remarkable for other qualities beside softness and weakness. It may be a mere chance conjunction, but it is at least remarkable, that the same age has given us in the three greatest departments of art—poetry, painting, and sculpture—women who, whatever be their faults or merits, are pre-eminently distinguished for one quality above all others, namely, strength. *Aurora Leigh* is perhaps the least "Angelical" poem in the language, and bears the relation to *Psyche* that a chiselled steel corslet does to a silk boddice with lace trimmings. The very hardness of its rhythm, its sturdy wrestlings and grapplings, one after another, with all the sternest problems of our social life—its forked-lightning revelations of character—and finally, the storm of glorified passion with which it closes in darkness (like nothing else we ever read since the mountain-tempest scene in *Childe Harold*)

—all this takes us miles away from the received notion of a woman's poetry.

And for Painting, let us look at Rosa Bonheur's canvas. Those droves of wild Highland black cattle, those teams of trampling Norman horses—do they belong to the same school of female art as all the washed-out saints, and pensive ladies, and graceful bouquets of Mesdemoiselles and Signorine Rosee, and Rosalba, and Panzacchi, and Grebber, and Mérian and Kauffman? We seem to have passed a frontier, and entered a new realm wherein Rosa Bonheurs are to be found.

Then for Sculpture. Will woman's genius ever triumph here? We confess we look to this point as to the touchstone of the whole question. Sculpture is in many respects at once the noblest art and the one which tasks highest both creative power and scientific skill. A really good and great statue is an achievement to which there must contribute more elements of power and patience than in almost any other human work, and it is, when perfected, one of the most sublime. We know generally very little of this matter in England. We possess pictures by the great masters sufficient in number and excellence to afford a fair conception (though of course an incomplete one) of the powers of painting. But notwithstanding the antique treasures in the Elgin and Arundel Collections, and a few fine modern statues to be found in private houses in this country, it is, I believe, to every one a revelation of a new agency in art when he first visits Italy and beholds the "Laocöon," the "Apollo," the "Niobe," and the "Psyche," of Praxiteles. Hitherto sculpture has appeared to be merely the production of beautiful forms, more or less true to nature. Now it is perceived to be genius breathing through form, the loftiest thoughts of human souls. "Apollo Belvidere" is not the mere figure of a perfect man in graceful attitude, as we thought it from casts and copies in England. It is Power itself, deified and made real before our eyes. The "Laocöon" is not the hapless high priest writhing in the coil of the serpent. It is the impersonation of the will of a giant man, a Prometheus struggling with indomitable courage against the resistless Fate in whose grasp meaner mortals are crushed helplessly. The "Niobe" is not merely a woman of noblest mould inspired by maternal anguish. She is glorified Motherhood, on whose great bosom we could rest, and round whose neck we could throw our arms. And the "Psyche" in the Museo Borbonico?—is this a poor fragment of a form, once perhaps graceful and fair, but now a mere ruin? No! It is the last gleam of the unknown glory of ancient art, the one work of human hands which we forget to admire because we learn to love it—the revelation to each of us of our innermost ideal of friend or wife, the sweetest, purest of our dreams made real before our eyes.

Not untruly has sculpture been named the *Ars*

*Divinior.* A deep and strange analogy exists between it and the highest we know of the Supreme Artist's works. Out of the clay, cold and formless, the sculptor slowly, patiently, with infinite care and love, moulds an image of beauty. Long the stubborn clay seems to resist his will, and to remain without grace or proportion, but at last the image begins, faintly and in a far-off way, to reflect that prototype which is in the sculptor's mind. The limbs grow into shape, and stand firmly balanced, the countenance becomes living and radiant. And last of all, the character of true sculpture appears; there is calm and peace over it all, and an infinite divine repose, even when the life within seems higher and fuller than that of mortality. The moulding is done, the statue is perfected.

But even then, when it should seem that the sculptor's great work is achieved, and that his image should be preserved and cherished evermore, what does he in truth do with his clay? Return hither, oh traveller, in a few short days, and the image of clay is gone, its place knows it no more. It has returned to the earth whence it was taken, thrown by, perchance for ever, or else kneaded afresh in some new form of life. Did he make it, then, but for destruction, and mould it so carefully but to crush it out at last in dust? Look around with illumined eyes! In the great studio of the universe the Divine image is still to be found, not now moulded in clay and ready to perish, dull of hue and dead in lustre, but sculptured in eternal marble, white, and pure, and radiant; meet to stand for ever in the palaces on high.

Sculpture is the noblest of the arts; nay, it is above all others in this very thing which has been pointed at as its bane and limitation. Its aim must ever be the expression of calmness and repose. No vehement wildness of the painter's dream, no storm of the musician's harmony, no ecstasy of the poet's passion; but the stillness and the peace of which earth knows so little. To bring our souls into sympathy with a great work of sculpturesque repose, is to bring them into the serener fields of the upper air, where the storms approach not, nor any clouds ascend. We do not naturally in the earlier moral life feel in union with things calm and still like these. The struggle in our own breasts, the lordly will wrestling with the lower powers for mastery, leaves us rather able to sympathize with all nature's warfare of wind and wave, all human death-battles, than with the repose in which the saint's soul rests, loving the cloudless sky and waveless sea, and the smile of a sleeping child nestled in the long sweet grass of summer. To reach that rest of the whole nature, which is at the same time absolute repose and absolute action of every power and every faculty in perfect balance, is the "Beulah land,"

> Where blessed saints dwell ever in the light
> Of God's dear love, and earth is heaven below.
> For never doubt nor sin may cloud their sight,
> And the great PEACE OF GOD calms every human woe.

The art which is the idealizing, the perpetuation of repose is, then, the divinest art—the art to be practised only by great souls,—great races of men. Egyptians and Greeks were races of sculptors; Hindoos and Mexicans stone-cutters of goblins. We repeat that the sharpest test to which the question of woman's genius can be put is this one of sculpture. If she succeed here, if a school of real sculpturesses ever arise, then we think that in effect the problem is solved. The greater includes the less. They may still fall below male composers in music, though we have seen some (inedited) music of wonderful power from a female hand. They may produce no great drama—perhaps no great historical picture. Yet if really good statues come from their studios, statues showing at once power of conception and science of execution, then we say, women can be artists. It is no longer a question whether the creative faculty be granted to them.

Now, we venture to believe that there are distinct tokens that this solution is really to be given to the problem. For long centuries women never seem to have attempted sculpture at all; perhaps because it was then customary for the artist to perform much of the mechanical labour of the marble-cutter himself; perhaps because women could rarely command either the large outlay or the anatomical instructions. But in our time things are changed. The Princesse Marie d'Orleans, in her well-known Joan of Arc, accomplished a really noble work of sculpture. Others have followed and are following in her path, but most marked of all by power and skill comes Harriet Hosmer, whose Zenobia (standing in the International Exhibition, in the same temple with Gibson's Venus) is a definite proof that a woman can make a statue of the very highest order. Whether we consider the noble conception of this majestic figure, or the science displayed in every part of it, from the perfect *pose* and accurate anatomy, to the admirable truth and finish of the drapery, we are equally satisfied. Here is what we wanted. A woman—ay, a woman with all the charms of youthful womanhood—can be a sculptor, and a great one.

Now we have arrived at a conclusion worthy of some little attention. Women, a few years ago, could only show a few weak and washy female poets and painters, and no sculptors at all. They can now boast of such true and powerful artists in these lines as Mrs. Browning, Rosa Bonheur, and Harriet Hosmer. What account can we give of the rise of such a new constellation? We confess ourselves unable to offer any solution, save that proposd by a gifted lady, to whom we propounded our query. Female artists, hitherto, have always started on a wrong track; being persuaded beforehand that they ought only to compose sweet verses and soft pictures, they set themselves to make them accordingly, and left us Mrs. Hemans' Works and Angelica's paintings. *Now*, women who possess any real genius, apply it to the creation of what they (and not society for them) really admire. A woman naturally admires power, force, grandeur. It is these qualities, then, which we shall see more and more appearing, as the spontaneous genius of woman asserts itself.

We know not how this may be. It is, at all events, a curious speculation. One remark we must make before leaving this subject. This new element of *strength* in female art seems to impress spectators very differently. It cannot be concealed that while all true artists recognise it with delight, there is no inconsiderable number of men to whom it is obviously distasteful, and who turn away more or less decidedly in feeling from the display of this or any other power in women, exercised never so inoffensively. There is a feeling (tacit or expressed) "Yes, it is very clever; but, somehow, it is not quite feminine." Now we do not wish to use sarcastic words about sentiments of this kind, or demonstrate all their unworthiness and ungenerousness. We would rather make an appeal to a better judgment, and entreat for a resolute stop to expressions ever so remotely founded on them. The origin of them all has perhaps been the old error that clipping and fettering every faculty of body and mind was the sole method of making a woman—that as the Chinese make a lady's foot, so we should make a lady's mind; and that, in a word, the old ale-house sign was not so far wrong in depicting "The Good Woman" as a woman without any head whatsoever.

Earnestly would we enforce the opposite doctrine, that as God means a woman to *be* a woman, and not a man, every faculty He has given her is a woman's faculty, and the more each of them can be drawn out, trained, and perfected, the more *womanly* she will become. She will be a larger, richer, nobler, woman for art, for learning, for every grace and gift she can acquire. It must indeed be a mean and miserable man who would prefer that a woman's nature should be pinched, and starved, and dwarfed, to keep on his level, rather than be nurtured and trained to its loftiest capacity, to meet worthily his highest also.

Thus we quit the subject of woman's pursuit of the Beautiful, rejoicing in the new promise of its success, and wishing all prosperity to the efforts to afford female students of art that sound and solid training, the lack of which has been their greatest stumbling-block hitherto. The School of Art and Design in London, is a good augury, with its eight hundred and sixty-three lady pupils!

But for woman's devotion to the True in physics and metaphysics, woman's science and woman's learning, what shall we venture to say? The fact must be frankly admitted—women have even more rarely the powers and tastes needful to carry them in this direction than in that of art. The love of abstract Truth as a real passion is probably antithetic in some measure to that vivid interest in persons which belongs to the warm sympathies and strong affections of women. Their quickness of perception militates against the slow toil of science, and their vividness of intuitive faith renders them often impatient of the discussions of philosophy. Many women love truth warmly enough, and for religious truth, female martyrs have never been wanting since the mother of the Maccabees. But few women complete their love of truth by such hatred of error as shall urge them to the exertion of laboriously establishing and defining the limits of the truths they possess. These natural causes, again, have been reinforced by endless artificial hindrances. The want of schools and colleges, the absence of such rewards as encourage (though they cannot inspire) the pursuit of knowledge, popular and domestic prejudices rendering study disfavoured, difficult access to books or leisure from household duties, the fluctuating health fostered by the unwholesome habits of women; and, lastly, the idleness and distractions of those very years of youth in which education can rise above the puerile instruction of a girls' schoolroom.

Far be it from us to wish to force all women into courses of severe study—to put (as has been well said of late) Arabian horses to the plough, and educate directly against the grain; only we desire thus much, that those women who do possess the noble love of knowledge and are willing to undergo the drudgery of its acquirement, should have every aid supplied and every stumbling-block removed from their paths. The improvements which in our time are making in these directions may be briefly stated. First, popular prejudice against well-educated women is dying away. It is found they do *not* "neglect infants for quadratic equations," nor perform in any way less conscientiously the various duties of life after reading Plato or even Kant. Secondly, the opening of ladies' colleges, such as Bedford-square and Harley-street, where really sound and solid instruction is given by first-rate teachers at a cost not equal to half that of the shallow and superficial boarding-schools of twenty years ago. Thirdly, women have benefited even more than men by the general progress of the times, the facilitation of travelling (formerly impossible to them without protection), the opening of good lending libraries, cheap books and postage. The dead sea of *ennui* in which so many of them lived is now rippled by a hundred currents from all quarters of heaven, and we may trust that the pettiness of gossip which has been the standing reproach of the sex will disappear with the narrowness of life which supplied no wholesomer food for conversation or thought. To cramp every faculty and cut off all large interests, and then complain that a human being so treated is narrow-minded and scandal-loving, is precisely an injustice parallel to that of some Southern Americans whom we have heard detail those vices of the negroes *which slavery had produced*, as the reason why they were justified in keeping so degraded a race in such a condition. It would be indeed a miracle often if a woman manufactured on some not unpopular principles were anything else than a very poor and pitiful piece of mechanism. The further improvements which may be sought in these directions are of various kinds. The standard of ordinary female education cannot perhaps be elevated above that of the ladies' colleges already mentioned, but *this* standard will become not (as now) the high-water mark for a few, but the common tide-line for all women of the middle and higher classes supposed to be fairly educated. Above this high standard, again, facilities and encouragements may be given to women of exceptionally studious tastes to rise to the level of any instruction attainable. One important way in which this last end may be reached—namely, the admission of women to the examinations and honours of the London University—has been lately much debated. The arguments which have determined its temporary rejection by the senate of the University (a rejection, however, only decided by the casting vote of the chairman), seem to have been all of the character discussed a few pages ago,—the supposed necessity of keeping women to their sole vocation of wives and mothers, and so on. The benefits which would accrue from the measure were urged by the present writer before the Social Science Congress,* and were briefly these—that women need

* *Female Education, and how it would be affected by University Examinations.* A Paper read before the Social Science Congress. Published by Emily Faithfull, Princes-street, Hanover-square. Price 2*d.* (Reprinted in the present volume.)

as much or more than men a stimulus to carry their education to a high pitch of perfection and accuracy; that this stimulus has always been supplied to men by university examinations and rewards of honour; that it ought to be offered to women, as likely to produce on them the same desirable results; lastly, that the University of London requiring no collegiate residence, and having its examinations conducted in special apartments, perfectly unobjectionable for women's use, it constitutes the one University in the kingdom which ought to admit women to its examinations.

Intimately connected with this matter is that of opening to women the medical profession, for which university degrees would be the first steps. The subject has been well worn of late; yet we must needs make a few remarks concerning it, and notably to put a question or two to objectors. Beloved reader (male or female, as the chance may be), did it ever happen to you to live in a household of half a dozen persons in which some woman was *not* the self-constituted family physician, to whom all the other members of the party applied for advice in ninety-nine cases out of a hundred? A cold, a cough, a rheumatism, a sprain, a cut, a burn, bile, indigestion, headaches and heartaches, are they not all submitted to her counsel, and the remedies she prescribes for them devoutly taken? Usually it is the grandmother or the housekeeper of the family who is consulted; but whichever it may chance to be, mistress or servant, it is always a *woman*. Who ever dreamed of asking his grandfather or his uncle, his butler or footman, "what he should do for this bad cold," or to "be so kind as to tie up this cut finger"? We can hardly imagine the astonishment of "Jeames" at such a request; but any woman abovestairs or below would take it as perfectly natural. Doctoring is one of the "rights of women," which albeit theoretically denied is practically conceded so universally that it is probable that all the M.D.'s in England, with the apothecaries to boot, do not order more drugs than are yearly "exhibited" by their unlicensed female domestic rivals. It is not a question whether such a state of things be desirable; it exists, and no legislation can alter it. The two differences between the authorized doctors and unauthorized doctoresses are simply these—that the first are paid and the second unpaid for their services, and the first have *some* scientific knowledge and the second none at all. It behoves us a little to consider these two distinctions. First, if patients choose to go for advice to women, and women inspire them with sufficient confidence to be consulted, it is a piece of interference quite anomalous in our day to prevent such services being rewarded, or in other words, to prevent the woman from qualifying herself legally to accept such reward. A woman may or may not be a desirable doctor, just as a dissenter may or may not be a desirable teacher; but unless we are to go back to paternal governments, we must permit patients and congregations to be the judges of what suits them best and not any medical or ecclesiastical corporation. It is not that *women* are called on to show cause why they should be permitted to enter the medical profession and obtain remuneration for their services, but the *doctors*, who are bound to show cause why they should exclude them and deprive them of the remuneration which there are abundance of patients ready to bestow. This is the side of the rights of the doctor. But are we not still more concerned with the second point of difference, which involves the safety of the patient? As we have said, men and women *will* go continually to women for medical advice in all those thousand contingencies and minor maladies out of which three-fourths of the mortal diseases of humanity arise. There is no use scolding, and saying they *ought* to go to the apothecary or the M.D. People will *not* do so least of all will delicate women do so when it is possible to avoid it. The only question is, whether the advice which in any case they will get from a woman will be good advice or bad advice—advice founded on some scientific knowledge, or advice derived from the wildest empiricism and crassest ignorance.

We have sometimes lamented that we have lacked the precaution of making memoranda of the wonderful remedies which have become known to us in the course of time, as applied by that class of domestic doctoresses of which we have spoken. They would have afforded a valuable storehouse of arguments to prove that, if "the little knowledge" of medicine (which we are told is all women could hope to acquire in a college) is a "dangerous thing," the utter absence of all knowledge whatever which they at present display, is a hundred times more perilous still. Well can we recall, for instance, in the home of our childhood, a certain admirable old cook who was the oracle in medical matters of the whole establishment. Notwithstanding the constant visits of an excellent physician, it was to her opinion that recourse was had on all emergencies; and the results may be imagined when it is avowed that in her genius the culinary and therapeutic arts were so assimilated, that she invariably *cooked* her patients as well as their dinners. On one occasion a groom having received an immense laceration and excoriation of the leg, was treated by having the wound *rubbed with salt, and held before a hot fire!*

At the opposite end of the social scale we can remember a lady of high degree and true Lady Bountiful disposition pressing on us, in succession, the merits of Morison's pills, hydropathy, and brandy and salt; "and if none of them cure your attack, there is St. John Long's remedy, which is *quite* infallible." It would not be easy to calculate how often such practitioners might incur the same chance as a grandmother of our own, who, asking an Irish labourer his name, received the *foudroyante* reply—"Ah! and don't you know me, my lady? And didn't your ladyship give the dose to my wife, and she died the next day?—*long life to your ladyship!*"

All this folly and quackery—nay, the use of quack medicines altogether—would be vastly diminished, if not stopped, by the training of a certain number of women as regular physicians, and the instruction derived through them of females generally, in the rudiments of physiology and sanitary science. It is vain to calculate whether individual lady physicians would be as successful as the ordinary average of male doctors. To argue about an untried capacity, *à priori*, seems absurd; and such experience as America has afforded us appears wholly favourable. But the point is, not whether women will make as good doctors as men, but how the whole female sex may be better taught in a matter of vital importance, not only to themselves, but to men whose health is modified through life by their mother's treatment in infancy. As the diffusion of physiological knowledge among women *generally* must unquestionably come from the instruction of a few women *specially* educated, the exclusion of females from courses of medical study assumes the shape of a decree that the sex on whom the health of the community peculiarly depends, shall for ever remain in ignorance of the laws by which that health is to be maintained.

With the highest possible education for women in

ladies' colleges, with University examinations and the medical profession opened to them, we have little doubt that new life would enter into many, and the pursuit of knowledge become a real vocation, where it has been hitherto hardly more than an amusement. Many a field of learning will yield unexpected flowers to a woman's fresh research, and many a path of science grow firm and clear before the feet which will follow in the steps of Mrs. Somerville. Already women have made for themselves a place, and a large one, in the literature of our time; and when their general instruction becomes deeper and higher, their works must become more and more valuable. Whether doctoresses are to be permitted or not, may be a question; but authoresses are already a guild, which, instead of opposition, has met kindliest welcome. It is now a real profession to women as to men, to be writers. Let any one read the list of books in a modern library, and judge how large a share of them were written by women. Mrs. Jameson, Mrs. Stowe, Miss Brontë, George Eliot, Mrs. Gaskell, Susan and Catherine Winkworth, Miss Martineau, Miss Bremer, George Sand, Mrs. Browning, Miss Procter, Miss Austen, Miss Strickland, Miss Pardoe, Miss Mulock, Mrs. Grey, Mrs. Gore, Mrs. Trollope, Miss Jewsbury, Mrs. Speir, Mrs. Gatty, Miss Blagden, Lady Georgiana Fullarton, Miss Marsh, and a dozen others. There is little need to talk of literature as a field for woman's future work. She is ploughing it in all directions already. The one thing is to do it thoroughly, and let the plough go deep enough, with good thorough drainage to begin upon. Writing books ought never to be thought of slightly. In one sense, it is morally a serious thing, a power of addressing many persons at once with somewhat more weight than in common speech. We cannot without offence misuse such a power, and adorn vice, or sneer at virtue, or libel human nature as all low, and base, and selfish. We cannot without offence neglect to *use* such a power for a good end; and if to give pleasure be the object of our book, make it at least to the reader an ennobling and refining pleasure. A book ought always to be *the high-water mark* of its author—his best thoughts, his clearest faith, his loftiest aspiration. No need to taunt him, and say he is not equal to his book. His book ought not to be merely the average of his daily ebb and flow, but his flood-line—his spring-tide jetsam of shells and corallines, and all "the treasures of the deep."

And again, writing is an Art, and as an art it should be seriously pursued. The true artist spirit which grudges no amount of preparatory study, no labour of final completion,—this belongs as much to the pen as to the pencil or the chisel. It is precisely this spirit which women have too often lacked, fondly imagining their quickness would do duty for patience, and their tact cover the defect of study. If their work is (as we hope and believe) to be a real contribution to the happiness and welfare of mankind hereafter, the first lesson to be learnt is this—conscientious preparatory study, conscientious veracity of expression, conscientious labour after perfection of every kind, clearness of thought, and symmetry of form. The time will come, we doubt not, when all this will be better understood. Writing a novel or a book of travels will not be supposed to come to a lady by nature, any more than teaching children to a reduced gentlewoman. Each art needs its special study and careful cultivation; and the woman who means to pursue aright either literature or science, will consider it her business to prepare herself for so doing, *at least* as much as if she purposed to dance on the stage, or make bonnets in a milliner's shop.

*Then*, we believe we shall find women able to carry forward the common progress of the human race along the path of the True, as well as of the Beautiful and the Good; nay, to give us those views of truth which are naturally the property of woman. For be it remembered, as in optics we need two eyes to see the roundness and fulness of objects, so in philosophy we need to behold every great truth from two stand-points; and it is scarcely a fanciful analogy to say, that these stand-points are provided for us by the different faculties and sentiments of men's and women's natures. In every question of philosophy there enters the intuitive and the experimental, the arguments *à priori* and *à posteriori*. In every question of morals there is the side of justice and the side of love. In every question of religion there is the idea of God as the Father of the world—the careful Creator, yet severe and awful Judge; and there is the idea of God as the Mother, whose tender mercies are over us all, who is grieved by our sins as our mothers are grieved by them, and in whose infinite heart is our only refuge. At the highest point all these views unite. Absolute Philosophy is both intuitive and experimental; absolute Morality is both justice and love; absolute Religion is the worship (at once full of awe and love) of the "Parent of Good, Almighty," who is both parents in One. But to reach these completed views we need each side by turns to be presented to us; and this can hardly be better effected than by the alternate action of men's and women's minds on each other.

# ESSAY IV.

## FEMALE CHARITY: LAY AND MONASTIC.

---

*Reprinted from Fraser's Magazine, December*, 1862.

---

WHATEVER else may be doubtful respecting woman's "general worth and particular missionariness," it is pretty well conceded that she is in her right place teaching the young, reclaiming the sinful, relieving the poor, and nursing the sick. Her pursuit of the True and the Beautiful in literature, science, and art, may be (however unjustly) derided as a failure or denounced as an invasion of fields which she can never adequately cultivate; but her pursuit of the Good, her efforts to ameliorate and brighten human life, have never been repudiated, and are daily more warmly recognised. Also, on the part of women themselves, there is a tendency, in nine out of ten, to choose one or other line of benevolent action, rather than any path of science, art, or learning. They love the beautiful, they distantly reverence the true; but a class of little children is better to them than a picture, and the recovery of a sick patient more interesting than the solution of a problem. Of the three great equal revelations of the Infinite One, the Good is open to all women at all times, the True and the Beautiful only exceptionally and by special grace. Of this pursuit, then, of the Good—or, in other words, of woman's philanthropy generally—we purpose to write a few pages, and notably of the prospects of such work in England at this time.

In a preceding article (*Fraser's Magazine*, November, 1862) we endeavoured to demonstrate that strenuous efforts ought to be made to open wider and more useful labours of different kinds to young women, thereby rendering their lives serviceable to the community and happy to themselves, and leaving them with no other motive to enter on marriage than the sole one which *ought* to decide them—namely, affection. We proceeded briefly to mention the manner in which such useful labours were now being opened to the humbler classes by the Society for the Employment of Women, the Victoria Press, Emigration Society, and other undertakings; and we then, at greater length, examined the prospects of the higher class of women, pursuing, freely, and with all needful instruction, the Beautiful in all the forms of art, and the True in the paths of science (especially of medical science) and of literature. The larger subject of their pursuit of the Good in philanthropy claimed full treatment by itself, and to this the present paper will be devoted. *So* large, indeed, is this theme, that we can do little more than indicate its general bearings, and then discuss the character of that important movement which promises shortly to revolutionize the charity of England—namely, the introduction of sisterhoods or deaconesses as recognised branches of the national church.

That Divine law which for ever evolves good out of evil, and makes the good durable and the evil evanescent, has never, perhaps, met a more remarkable realization than in the history of the Crimean War and its results in Russia and England. Of that terrible struggle which once filled all our thoughts and covered our land with mourning, what now remains? Some doubtful political results, a few headstones, growing mossy already, on Cathcart's Hill, and some tender memories in silent hearts. The world's interest has passed to other struggles and other climes, and the names of the Crimean martyrs, once in all men's mouths, are almost forgotten for those of the heroes of India and of Italy. But one result *has* survived, and is daily gaining wider significance. Those sanguinary battles, those far more terrible mismanaged lazar-houses and transports for the wounded and plague-stricken, were the origin of a movement whose limit it is hard to calculate. The hospital of Scutari was the cradle of a new life for the women of England, and (marvellous to relate) the hospital of Sebastopol served the same noble purpose for the women of Russia. In both countries, up to that period, the adoption by ladies (not members of Romanist or Greek orders) of any philanthropical tasks of a public kind had been altogether exceptional. Mrs. Fry, Mrs. Hannah More, and Miss Carpenter, had carried on their labours here, and for all we know, there were parallels for them in Russia; but till the cry of agony from the Crimea came to call forth Miss Nightingale's band and their sister nurses in the hostile camp, the "public function of woman" was still to be sought. A thousand prejudices did that gallant little army break down for ever. A new and noble lesson for all their sex did they bring back from that holy Eastern pilgrimage—that Woman's Crusade. When the Russian ladies returned to St. Petersburgh, and the English to London, they did more than keep up their own devotion to the sick and suffering, and found new institutions. They spread through the length and breadth of both lands a thought which we need not fear will ever be suffered to die out again—the thought that it is a woman's province to do good, to devote herself (when no home duty or special gift call her elsewhere) to relieve the miseries of mankind, and that it is to be *more* and not *less* a woman to go forth bravely to the task, undeterred by the cobweb conventionalities of an age which is rapidly passing away. We are persuaded that there is not a parish in broad England which somehow has not benefited by this thought; and in Russia we have been assured it is the same. Everywhere women have been inspired to perform their duties in relieving poverty, nursing the sick, and educating children; and a Russian lady who, twenty years ago, never dreamed of entering the cottage of a serf, now visits her poor and teaches in her schools as naturally as the wife or daughter of an English squire. We know of few things in history more beautiful than this legacy of charity left us by a miserable and sanguinary war.

From the departure of the nurses to the Crimea we thus date the beginning of English modern female philanthropy. Of course it existed in a measure before that time, and of course other causes have combined to aid its development since that period; but a new era very manifestly then commenced. With this modern phase of the subject we have to concern ourselves now—its present state and future prospects. It is no longer the work of half a dozen exceptional women labouring unaided save by men; it is the chosen life-task of hundreds—perhaps we should say of thousands—of women seeking to co-operate with one another. It is no longer small departments of the great field which are being worked by district visitors and Sunday-school teachers and young ladies going their rounds in their fathers' villages; it is the whole vast realm of suffering and want and sin in our land, wherein women are praying to be permitted to labour, and where they already are beginning to labour not wholly ineffectually. What chances may there be of good result from these efforts? Will the aid of woman essentially strengthen the hand of man in the battle—or, as some would tell us, only hamper and shackle him? We think there are fair grounds in the nature of the case for no small hopes.

It is not often those who concern themselves deeply with theories of evil, more or less good or sound, who practically do much in the world to lift its weight: the simple nature which takes no wide view of the universe, and grapples with no profound problem of existence, is often touched to its depths by some sight of actual misery, some individual or half-score cases of want, oppression, or suffering, brought before it: straightway the effort to relieve the pain or redress the wrong becomes the first step in a path of charity which opens out wider and wider for the rest of life. We believe this to be almost the invariable *rationale* of all successful schemes of beneficence. They have not originated from wide philosophic views and broad plans for the relief of mankind. Such things of course sometimes exist, and prosper and accomplish their noble ends. But far more frequently it is the other way—the grain of mustard-seed brings forth a "tree," while "the mountain falling cometh to naught."

Thus, the ordinary propensity of women to concern themselves with the concrete rather than the abstract —to care deeply for persons and little for theories,— tends to direct them to practical philanthropy with special advantage. They start from the right end —from small beginnings, whereby experience may be acquired step by step, and where the grand requisite is present of *individual* care and sympathy for each person concerned.

It would be a vain task to attempt to give any definite account of the work which women have been doing in England since the date of the Crimean war, which we have fixed as that of the new era of female philanthropy. Every few months some book, like *English Hearts and Homes; Ragged Homes, and How to Mend Them; Haste to the Rescue,* and many more, appears to open up some new field in process of culture. Criminals, old and young, male and female; released prisoners; the ragged school class; the industrial school class; drunkards; fallen women; girls in danger of falling to be saved by preventive missions; mothers who can be made to attend work meetings; the night school class, the adult school class, the class accessible by Bible women; navvies; factory girls; able-bodied paupers; the insane; idiots; blind, deaf, and dumb; the sick in free hospitals; the sick poor in their homes; the sick in workhouses; the incurables; the convalescents; women needing employment, women desiring to emigrate;—all these have the devotion of bands of philanthropists, of whom a large portion are women.

Now, if we consider the two terms of the question —a vast amount of new and untried work, and a vast number of new and unpractised workers—it will be clear enough that at the outset much confusion must exist, and much difficulty in getting "the right woman in the right place." Some work will need aid, and for a time be unable to obtain it; some women will desire to work, and be unable to find it to do. Bad machinery will be tried to the injury of much earnest labour; and wisely planned systems will fail from the employment of bad tools. The marvel to any one who knows a little of the present condition of philanthropy in England, is, not that there are failures and imperfections, and schemes starting up and dying down like mushrooms every year; it is that, amid all the elements of confusion, all the direful sectarian jealousies, all the poor selfish vanities and interests which, alas! must taint the holiest of human efforts, there is so *much* done—so much hopefully and steadily falling into order.

But the inevitable imperfections and delays in the new philanthropy cause bitter impatience among some of the most earnest workers. The modern principle of association, by which most of the schemes are carried on—the machinery of committees, secretaries, subscription lists and reports, provokes them continually by its grinding and clogging, and occasionally by its stopping and breaking up in the hands of the all unpractised engineers. Nay, worse! To carry on our simile, the stokers who have engaged to feed the engine, too often absent themselves on one pretext or another; and the whole train comes to a stand still while the ladies of the acting committee are gone to Switzerland and Italy, the principal subscribers have transferred their donations to a new charity, and the honorary secretary is going to be married. The ladies' committees alone seem to be a source of inextinguishable worry—all parties seeming to forget that some knowledge of the working of such things, some general habit of business *versus* aimless talk, is needful to make such meetings useful; and that even with such knowledge and business habits, the committees of gentlemen (*e. g.*, of the boards of guardians) are not always models of sagacity and moderation. Out of this discontent and impatience with the present machinery of philanthropy, comes the desire to introduce a different one, to substitute regular troops for volunteers who may be missing or married when most needed, and the good firm rule of a recognised Mother Superior for the vagaries of ladies' committees and the illicit omnipotence of an honorary secretary. The old argument between freedom and absolutism, between constitutional and despotic governments, has to be fought out here also. The failures of the self-governed will be brought up as testimonies to the superiority of "paternal" rule for many a year to come, before it be finally recognised that the failures of the one, ever tending to correct themselves, are better than the successes of the other, ever tending to deteriorate all concerned, whether the rulers or the ruled.

Other causes aiding, this desire of enthusiastic philanthropists to exchange the machinery of lay association for that of monastic orders, seems in process of being realized before long. The few Protestant convents established some years ago, and regarded with very general distrust and even odium, are now being rapidly multiplied; and the principle on which they are founded has met with an approbation perfectly astonishing to those who recall the former prejudice against them of all except the extreme section of the High Church party. In the Convocation of Canterbury for 1862, all orders of the clergy and all shades of theologic opinion were for once unanimous, and passed their solemn approval on the proposal that women adopting the vocation of charity should receive the formal sanction of the Church. Again, in the Church Congress at Oxford, in July of this same year, emphatic applause was lavished on the scheme. We have every reason to suppose that ere long some order, whether of nuns or deaconesses, will form a recognised branch of the National Church.

Should these anticipations prove true, a revolution must take place in philanthropic work in England. The principle of Lay Association and Monasticism will not, we apprehend, work well side by side; and in any case the monastic system will introduce enormous changes. Hitherto the work has been advancing with marvellous rapidity, and (in our humble opinion) with a constant progress towards more perfect organization of its own kind, such organization, namely, as is consistent with the principle of lay association. On the question of whether such lay organization would ever reach the point of being actually the *best* possible machinery for effecting the work to be accomplished, it is in vain to speculate. At least no one can be justified in affirming that it would never do so; nay, that it would not ere long become better than any other yet known.* But it would appear that a different experiment is to be tried by those who are impatient of the slow adaptation of the modern machinery. We are to go back to an older system—try the stage coaches again, since the railways so often break down. For the present, we are called off from examining the results and prospects of lay association, to consider the probabilities of greater success in the monastic system. It is certainly a remarkable and anomalous attempt thus to reproduce it, and will perhaps be one fraught with important

* A striking instance of the results which may be expected from the principle of Lay Association will be found in a book shortly to be published, a Life of Miss Sieveking, of Hamburg, edited by Miss C. Winkworth. It is the more remarkable because Miss Sieveking's own preferences had been in favour of the opposite principle, and her most cherished early dream had been that of founding a Protestant Sisterhood of Mercy. Yet the practical force of circumstances induced her in after-life to relinquish this scheme and found in its place a Lay Society, which carried into action some of the largest and best-worked plans of philanthropy in existence, and became the parent of similar associations in Denmark, Germany, Switzerland, and Russia.

consequences. Let us endeavour to give the subject the fairest investigation in our power. To do this we must go somewhat far back.

The fundamental principle of monasticism is not charity, but *asceticism*. Monasteries were not originally started to enable the monks to benefit the world, but to secure their own sanctification. This may be proved historically. The further back we ascend the less we find of charity, and the more of asceticism, till in the first centuries of Christian monasticism we come on no trace of charityat all. When the deserts of the Thebaïd were peopled by Anthony's hermits and Cyril's monks; when the Syrian plains could show their hundred Stylites, and their Boskoï, or "grazing monks," who fed in the fields like cattle; when Jerusalem possessed its madhouse (probably the first in the world) destined solely for monks driven crazed by austerities; when St. Syncletica and St. Marcella had filled east and west with nuns imitating all the savage mortifications of the monks, there was yet no Charitable Order, and no attempt to turn monastic fraternities to purposes of charity. In other creeds beside the Christian it was the same. The Brahmin Sunnyasi, the Buddhist Fakir, the Jewish Essene, the Peruvian Mamaçonas of the Sun, the Arab Dervish, all sought their own beatitude, *Niwane*, Paradise, not any benefit to their fellows. Not till the Crusades called forth the Religieuses Hospitalières and the nuns of the Holy Trinity contemporaneously with the chivalric orders of men, was there any monastic order devoted to the purposes of charity. And to the present day, among the ostensibly charitable orders the ascetic spirit is never wholly absent. On this we shall have more to say hereafter. At present, all we desire is to call attention to the fact that monastic institutions were not primarily founded on philanthropy (as Protestants often imagine), but on the wholly opposite principle of asceticism. Whether this original principle can ever be eliminated from the system is an open question. The experience of the existing Protestant convents looks the other way.

To understand the importance of this distinction of principles on which we desire to insist, a few words must be said regarding asceticism generally, and the reasons will then be manifest why we so urgently deprecate its intervention in English philanthropy. Asceticism is logically founded on the doctrine of two moralities, an exoteric morality for the multitude, consisting of adherence to the eternal moral law, and an esoteric morality for those who aspire to special sanctity, consisting of self-denial in things lawful, and supererogatory "works" over and above the demands of the law. The doctrine that any such double morality exists, is in itself false and baneful in the highest degree. The eternal and immutable moral law of the universe, which is identical with the Will of God, demands of every moral agent the very best and highest action and sentiment possible in each particular case. No better or higher *can* exist, for the moment any one is apprehended to be so, it becomes imperative duty. It is to degrade the law of absolute right, absolute truth, absolute purity, to suppose a higher right, or truth, or purity. This is the theoretical error of asceticism. Practically it has two aspects, the religious and the moral. On the religious side it assumes such supererogatory works and mortifications to be especially pleasing to God. Our Maker, it is supposed, demands of all men justice and truth, and to refrain from murder, adultery, and the like. But he who would really please God and prove his devotion to Him, must go beyond such moral duties, and *give God something*—his own life, or that of his children, his cattle, or his gold. In early times and barbarous countries, where God was believed to be a cruel and sanguinary Being, it naturally followed that the more cruel were the sacrifice, the more pleasing it was supposed to be in His sight. Here was the origin of the bloody rites of Moloch and Juggernaut, and of the self-tortures of the priests of Baal and the Flagellants. In later and milder creeds the sacrifice was mitigated, and the nun of our day sacrifices her affections, the Jesuit his free will. One and all give to the Lord of Goodness oblations which are abominations in His sight.

On the moral side, asceticism represents self-mortification as a species of spiritual exercise or gymnastic, conducive to self-conquest and excelling sanctity.

Here has been the origin of perhaps even wider, though less glaring, evils than religious asceticism, by tempting thousands of the noblest souls in all lands and ages to strive to climb up to virtue by a path which never has led thither, and from whose barren and herbless cliffs they either rise into clouds of spiritual pride, or fall down and are lost in gulphs of sensualism below. Both the religious and moral sentiments on which asceticism takes hold, are in themselves noble and holy, and the aberrations to which they have given existence are too sad and mournful to be calmly contemplated. It is a noble thing to desire to please God at the cost of pain and suffering to ourselves; a holy and *true* feeling that we ought to sacrifice body and soul to Him. The instinct is so pure and strong, that in lives of great ease and happiness it often seems as if some mode of expressing it in self-denial *must* be found. But the error is in imagining that that rightful sacrifice *can* be paid in any other way than "the reasonable, holy, and acceptable sacrifice" of a life of love to Him and to our neighbour;—that we can please Him by breaking the laws He has given to our bodies and minds, and not by cheerful obedience to them all. Cicero said well, "Men think to please the gods by mutilating their bodies, but if they desired to anger them, what else could they do?" Shall we please a mechanist by shattering his machine; a musician by untuning his instrument? But vainly have prophets and apostles proclaimed what pure religion and undefiled really demands, while the old idolatrous and demonolatrous ideas still linger on and are preached on every side. After three thousand years, Christendom still believes that God *does* desire more of man than "to do justice, and love mercy, and walk humbly with his God."

And the moral sentiment of asceticism is no less noble than the religious. The "thirst after righteousness," the desire to stretch out after the very purest holiness, and not resting content with ordinary goodness, to achieve perfection even through any sufferings and privations, to struggle on

> "Till the lordly will o'er its subject powers
> Like a thronèd God prevail"—

this is a glorious thing—an ambition worthy of an immortal soul. To seek this perfection of holiness, this absolute self-conquest, *by self-mortification*, is the error of the intellect which chooses the wrong path, not of the will which has chosen the right end.

Even in its gloomiest phases, when asceticism fixes itself on guilt, and becomes the longing for expiation, it is a sacred thing. He who has never known what it is to desire his own punishment, knows but little of repentance. But here also there is error. There is enormous presumption (though the ascetic sees it not) in the idea that man may be his own judge and executioner—his own physician in the sickness of his soul.

Such, then, is the principle of asceticism, and such,

we conceive, the errors on which it is founded. There is, indeed, extant historical evidence that the doctrine of the higher and lower morality was the proximate cause of Christian monastic asceticism.

"In the second century," says Mosheim (*Eccles. Hist.* B. I., Cent. 2, Chap. iii.), "was started a principle in morals, radically false and most injurious to the Christian cause, but one that has in every age, even to our own, been infinitely prolific in evil. Christian doctors maintained that Christ had prescribed a two-fold rule of holiness and virtue: the one ordinary, for men of business; the other extraordinary, for men of leisure and such as sought to obtain higher glory in the future world. They applied the name of *Precepts* to those laws which are universally obligatory; but the *Counsels* concerned only those who aimed at a closer union with God. On a sudden there arose, accordingly, a class of persons who professed to strive after that higher and more eminent holiness than common men can attain. They thought many things forbidden to them which are allowed to other Christians, such as wine, flesh, matrimony, and worldly business. They supposed they must emaciate their bodies with watching, fasting, toil, and hunger. Both men and women imposed these hard conditions on themselves. They thus obtained the name of ascetics, eclectics, she-philosophers. (Clemens Alex. calls them ἐκλέκτων ἐκλεκτότεροι, the more elect among the elect.) Those of this century who embraced this life did not altogether withdraw from society. In process of time, however, they retired into the deserts, and afterwards formed associations, taking pattern by the Essenes and Therapeutæ."

The results of the acceptance of the ascetic principle in religion are twofold—the desecration of common life and natural relations, on the one hand; and on the other, the mistaken pursuit of superior holiness by a method which leads to no such result.

It is a good observation of Archbishop Whately, that the boast of the sanctity and learning preserved in the monasteries during the Middle Ages, amounts to much less than at first sight appears. When every man and woman inspired with a little more piety than usual was invited to display it, *not* by performing the natural duties of family and station, and so improving society, but by renouncing family and station, and leaving society to shift for itself, it is small marvel that the world, forsaken by all its best spirits, appeared exceedingly bad, and the monasteries, where all such spirits were congregated, exceedingly good in comparison. A gentleman having gone round his house, and taken the lamps and candles out of the drawing-room, the library, the picture gallery, and the kitchen, and collected them all in the cellar, might with equal justice call on his neighbours to remark how dark was the house, how beautifully illuminated the cellar!

Nor is it solely by taking the best spirits out of it that monasticism desecrates society. It leaves those who remain in it with the impression that no such high standard of goodness is demanded of them as of those formally dedicated to piety or charity. Thus family ties come to be looked on, not as the most blessed helps which God has given us on our upward path, but almost as hindrances, as clogs upon the soul, which may rise higher by casting them off. Thus all necessary industry or pursuit of art or science, instead of being ennobled by the belief that it is "that state of life to which it has pleased God to call us," and as fit as any other, therefore, to be religiously followed, come, on the contrary, to be placed in antithesis to a religious vocation, and are desecrated accordingly.

On the other hand, those who renounce the natural joys and duties of life, to follow out the principle of asceticism, find themselves no nearer to virtue or peace of mind. The principle is of illimitable application. It is better to fast all day than half the day, to watch all night than half the night, better to be a Trappist than a priest, better a Stylites than a Trappist. At every stage of self-mortification there is another yet stricter and more savage, appealing with the same motive to the devotee. The condition of a conscience which should logically carry out such a principle is too piteous to think of; and though this is doubtless rather the theoretical than the actual result of asceticism in all save exceptional cases, yet much of the evil must exist. No one who thinks it better or more pleasing to God to deny himself natural pleasures than to enjoy them, can ever know the peace of heart of a simple thankful acceptance of the order of Providence alike for pain or pleasure. Nor is the spiritual condition of the ascetic in other ways a more healthful one. The constant self-introspection which his system enforces, is as little likely to produce soundness of mind and conscience, as the habits of the hypochondriac to produce soundness of body, when he shuts himself in his heated chamber with his finger on his pulse, trying his own fanciful remedies, when all he needs is air and work. All that is noble in human nature comes from the *centrifugal* force within us, carrying us out of and above ourselves in pure love of God and man, for goodness, beauty, truth. All that is mean and false and sickly comes of the centripetal force of *selfism,* bringing us back to our own poor feelings and interests. Instead of ascending to a higher virtue through a training which forces us to think of ourselves continually, we are clipping the wings by which God meant us to soar. Let us ponder the judgment of the system of one who tried it in all the severity of discipline of the Devonport Sisterhood, and gave it up at last, because, in the true and noble work of the Eastern hospitals, she had learned to understand its fallacy. After describing the extreme austerities of the order, Miss Goodman says (*Experiences of an English Sister of Mercy,* p. 7):*

* Several attempts have been made by the friends of monasticism to detract from the value of Miss Goodman's testimony on

"Setting aside the question whether such a life causes us to neglect social duties, it is doubtful whether it really trains the soul to any high degree of holiness, or is elevating to the character. It appeared to some who watched it to have the effect of narrowing the sympathies, of engendering ignorance, self-conceit, and spiritual pride, and of altogether destroying simplicity and self-forgetfulness. . . . . I have heard ladies acquainted with the conventual life remark that nuns, as a class, exhibit much petty selfishness and self-complacency; yet the nun's waking hours are supposed to be spent almost entirely in thinking over her sins. She examines herself and re-examines herself—in short, so trains her mind to dwell upon herself, that at last she has no control of her thoughts. Thus all her little concerns become so magnified that she will shed floods of tears if her cap be starched too stiffly."

And again, regarding abstinence from natural food, which is always, by some fatality, made the first merit of asceticism, as if the Gnostic blasphemy were true, and the Creator of the world were an evil Being, whose bounteous gifts we should please the true God by rejecting with disdain,—Miss Goodman says of its moral results (and we believe that the experi-

the subject. The facts and conclusions, however, quoted in the present paper, have never been answered in any way. We have no doubt that Miss Goodman's forthcoming book will meet all other objections satisfactorily.

ence of all who have tried it will corroborate her judgment):—

"I cannot tell why it is supposed that fasting, besides being a mortification, is likely to prove a means of making us indifferent to the promptings of the flesh; why it is thought that, under such circumstances, the soul should be less dragged down by the body, and therefore capable of higher flights. I have heard those who have tested this by experience say, that during a severe fast, when walking the streets, engaged in work, in church, or wherever they might be, their thoughts would run off from that in which they ought to be occupied, and in imagination they were counting the loaves in some baker's shop, or something of that kind."—(P. 6.)

A friend of our own, who once carried such practices extremely far, gave this very remarkable testimony of their results:—

"I think the chief effects were that I thought only of myself, and that I grew very hard-hearted towards my fellow-creatures. Instead of feeling for the poor and suffering as I used to do, I came to think, 'Well, after all, they are not more uncomfortable than I am.'"

Nay, the results of the dire mistake of asceticism are not merely negative—the privation of natural joy and progress towards a healthy virtue—they have produced, under the Romish system, evils too dreadful to be spoken of now,—evils which are hardly to be studied in the books which have ventured to disclose them. We will but quote one testimony—that of Blanco White—speaking of the years during which he was confessor to many nunneries in Seville:—

"I have, in the course of my life, come in contact with characters of all descriptions. I have seen human nature at various stages of elevation and debasement, but *souls* more polluted than some of the professed vestals of the Church of Rome never fell within my observation."—(*Life*, vol. i. p. 70.)

If such be the moral results of asceticism—if it fail thus deplorably to produce that high virtue at which it aims—what shall we say of its results on the *happiness* of mankind? If that high virtue were really attained, we might perchance be enabled to contemplate, with some mournful assent, the pain it has wrought. But, as the case stands, what shall save the whole system from bearing the execration due to the source of all that mass of misery which has been accumulating in the convents of Europe for thirteen centuries? What have the warm loving hearts of women suffered in their nunneries, cut off not only from life and freedom, but from all those affections which are the life of life to woman! We are not speaking now of penances and tortures, of "*in paces*" where the victims were buried alive, or of tremendous "rules" whereby the poor, weak frames are kept in constant pangs of hunger and sleeplessness, all the Divine laws of health being set aside; where the bodies

God has so "wonderfully made" to praise Him by their beauty, and do His work with willing hands, are degraded by uncleanness, torn by the lash or excoriated by the penitential *cilicium*;* where the minds themselves of the devotees are destroyed by perpetual silence, till, as in the old heathen fable, the hideous transformation is repeated, and women are changed into the likeness of gibbering birds.† We are not speaking now of these more severe excesses, only of the ordinary convents, with their life-long imprisonments and separation from all human interests and affections.

It has been truly said, there is a worse hell than the hell of suffering—it is the hell of *ennui*; the endless, hopeless, leaden monotony of a living grave like this.

* Here is a cell of a nun of St. Theresa (Carmelite), described by an eye-witness: "Each bed consists of a wooden plank raised in the middle, and on days of penitence crossed by wooden bars. The pillow is wooden. The nun lies on this couch with her feet hanging out, as the bed is made too short on principle. Round her waist she wears a band with iron points turned inwards. After having scourged herself with a whip with iron nails, she lies down for a few hours on the wooden bars, and rises at four o'clock."—*Mexico*, p. 223, by Madame C. de la Barca.

† In the Sepolte Vive, in Rome, the recluses observe almost eternal silence. Of the results we are enabled to form an estimate from the testimony of a lady who obtained the Pope's permission to spend six hours in their convent, during which their rule was relaxed. It appeared that among young and old a sort of dotage had supervened. They were not so much unhappy as idiotic. For the six hours they all jabbered incessantly, simultaneously, without listening to anything, and nearly without meaning.

Who may guess the agonies with which a human being, awakened out of the fanaticism or the despair which drove it into such a dungeon, should clamour for escape, should beat its bars like a prisoned brute struggling for liberty! But no! There is no tyrant's dungeon better guarded, with higher walls and stronger locks, than this "*happy*" convent of holy women! The effort, nay, the wish, to escape (confessed, as it soon must be) will but bring tenfold penance. And then the poor wretch turns in despair—to whom? Not to her once smooth-tongued superior; she is her tyrant now. Not to her fellow-prisoners; a nun has no right to have a friend, and can rarely trust one not to betray her. Not to the loving hearts outside—the sister, father, mother, who would give their lives for hers, who are only a few miles, perhaps a few paces, away. The walls rise up before her eyes and shut them out for ever. Shall she turn to God? But who is that dread Being whom to propitiate she has cast herself into this gulf of misery, and in whose name she is chained in its depths? That is not God—not the God any heart can love.

And all this wretchedness unspeakable has been going on for ages, in tens of thousands of souls, for whom life has been one long agony. And now we are called on to revive Monasticism!—to look to its restoration as an event of happy augury!

How does all this apply to English Protestant nunneries? Simply so far that we believe, though in the minds of their advocates the *utility* of such institutions is their recommendation, yet latent beneath there must always survive that asceticism which was the origin of the system, and which may, at any moment, crop out again, and cause evils as nearly parallel to those of old as the free laws of England may render possible. We believe that we are justified in this assertion by the actual history of the more important of the convents yet tried in this country. Again we must quote the revelations in Miss Goodman's book. Here is the instructive history of the Devonport Anglican Convent:—

"Miss Sellon, deeply moved by the wretchedness of the poor, determined to devote her little fortune, together with what other talents God had given her, to the relief of misery. With this intention, in 1847, she came to Stoke, part of Devonport, where she lived in humble lodgings. After a short time, being joined by another lady, a small house was taken, and the two continued working among the poor in all simplicity. . . . . In 1859 the Society consisted of about twenty ladies, divided into three orders. The sister of the order of the Sacred Heart wore but one under-garment, a long, rough flannel chemise, no stockings, and sandals in the place of shoes. The daily rule was as follows:—Rise at three A. M., then alternations of prayer, work, and self-examination, till ten, when came the long-looked-for breakfast, in which dinner was included. . . . . I have said that this rule was modified with regard to the outer orders; yet it was elevated above all usefulness, and held up as the perfection of holy living, the rule of almost perpetual silence being evidently in view for both orders. One lady arrived at such a perfection of speechlessness, that she had not spoken for several years, except to the superior or senior sister, at rare intervals. . . . . One of the strictest rules of a nun's life is, that she walk loose to all human friendships; she must consider all ties of relationship severed when she becomes a recluse, and, therefore, she drops her surname, and often assumes a new Christian name. Whether at Miss Sellon's or any other nunnery, if a friendship between two of the members be discovered, they are at once carefully separated. But in sickness I have often observed that the love of her childhood's home, and the brothers and sisters who dwelt there with her, often rushes back to the heart of the nun with tenfold force, on account of the isolation hitherto imposed. A dying sister, at Plymouth, said, 'I sit and think of home till I fear I am going mad. Go and request Sister —— to come to me, that I may ask the lady superior to let me go home while I have strength: I cannot die without seeing my father.' She *did*, poor creature, about a month after the declaration."—(*Experiences*, pp. 2, 13.)

Who will dare to tell us, after this, that the convents of England are secure from the curse of Romish asceticism?

There are other, though less important, sides of the Monastic question, beside asceticism, which it now behoves us to consider. With reference to its introduction on a large scale in England, it is manifest that several results would follow, especially concerning the state of things here, and the character and position of English women. Of these we must speak as briefly as possible.

One of the greatest achievements of modern philanthropy has been the obliteration of much sectarian prejudice and rancour. Men united in the same heartfelt desire to relieve human misery, cease, in a degree, to remember their theologic differences; and we have at last beheld in our Social Science Congresses the truly blessed sight of Churchmen and Dissenters, Protestants and Catholics, Calvinists and Unitarians, working cordially hand in hand. It cannot but be dreaded that the establishment of charitable orders in the Church of England will introduce fresh difficulties and bring out differences which might have become forgotten. The work of a *society* needs only co-operation; the work of an *order* needs uniformity. A new spirit of party and cabal may rise up to disturb the new hopes of harmony among English philanthropists. Already, as we have learned, in France the fraternity of St. Vincent de Paul exercises a most obnoxious sway throughout the country, placing a social stigma upon any lady who refuses to subscribe to their funds. And in Germany a significant incident proves that

Protestant fraternities will not be exempt from the same spirit of cabal. The "religious interest" of Berlin was at once brought to bear in favour of the nomination of a Kaiserswerth deaconess to the position of professor in the hospital of the *Charité*, notoriously earned, by the most laborious study, by that remarkable woman, Marie Zakrzewska (*vide, A Practical Illustration of Woman's Right to Labour*, p. 60). But in truth we need no instances to convince us of results too accordant with all experience of confraternities.

Again: communities and families are naturally antithetic to each other. There is for ever a tendency in each to break up the other. Wherever the natural and excellent association of two friends or sisters enlarges itself into a community, the evil begins, and others are tempted to join whose family duties should have kept them at home. We would not exaggerate this objection. So many women remain helplessly when youth is past in homes where they are not wanted, to the loss of all usefulness in life, that it would even seem as if the opening of nunneries for them would, in some respects, cut the knot of their small difficulties, and prove a benefit. But there is all the difference imaginable between a woman leaving her home for free work, and leaving it to join a community where all her ties of blood are changed for the ties of an artificial community. Perhaps this *need* not be so; but assuredly the tendency has never hitherto been escaped. What has been the result of every convent in the world but this transference? What does it mean to give up the father's or husband's name, which ought to be dear and sacred to every daughter or widow, and become henceforth only Sister Mary or Sister Catherine, as if the family was to be nothing, and the community everything? What does it mean using all these old words to distinguish the convent from the home, with its mother-superior, and sisters, and cells, and refectory, and all the rest of the paraphernalia of a system which was founded on the ascetic distinction between the world and the Church? What does it mean, the adoption of the special garb which shall mark the sister as having ceased to hold the social position to which she was born, and to belong to a community? We would not speak hastily of these things. If to romantic imaginations there are certain false attractions about convent names, and rules, and dresses, of a puerile and contemptible kind, there are, doubtless, on the other hand, very real ones to a devout mind in the idea of a definite and complete dedication of the whole life to God in a manner so manifest to all as to leave no loophole for the worldly spirit ever to claim them again. The abode, the name, the garb, which should at every moment recall such dedication, would seem dear as to a soldier his flag and uniform. But there is another side of the question which ought not to be forgotten. That garb and name which should stamp the wearer as dedicated to God's service, sets up at once that claim of special holiness which is false in itself and the poison of all simplicity of action. It is sad enough that *religion* should be a professional matter with our clergy, with its conventional dress and conventional morals, destroying, as they so often do, the influence of the most honest among them. But grievous will be the pity if *charity* also becomes a profession, and dons its garb, and assumes its conventional style. We are not advocating affected secresy about philanthropic work. If much good is to be done, some publicity must needs attend it. The right hand must keep itself to its own pocket if it may never take the left into council. But there is a long way between this and the formal adoption of philanthropy as a sacred profession, an experiment which cannot fail to be fraught with many perils.

We are called on to admire the propriety and modesty of conventual attire. Surely English women need not go back to the morality which should stigmatize all beauty and variety of costume (as the Fathers did), as if it were the result of evil desires? It is an insult to the honour of all women to be told that a veil and black robe are more "modest" than their ordinary dress. It is a piece of rank asceticism to mark off the supposed special sanctity of the task by the special gloom of the attire. We have heard of a great artist, the most simple-minded of men, solemnly remonstrating with an Anglican nun on the ugliness of her dress, its concealment of her hair, &c. He evidently imagined that proving it to be *ugly* was sufficient to condemn it. That anyone could of *malice prepense* make a dress gloomy and unbecoming, was a a thing undreamed of in his philosophy. And was he not right? Why *should* human creatures render themselves disagreeable to the sight of their fellows, or renounce any natural charms or graces? If this question be pressed home, we apprehend some startling views of the origin of all such practices will come to light. It is a suspicious feature in any religious system when it tends to throw the minds of its votaries into antagonism with the order of Providence. The Creator of this world assuredly loves beauty, and lavishes it over all His works in endless variety. The worshipper who should be most fully imbued with His spirit would hardly choose in preference either a gloomy or monotonous garb or abode. God clothes no flower in black, and teaches no bird to build itself a cell.

Conventual dress seems a very trivial matter, but there is no point of the system which more betrays to a thoughtful mind the ascetic principle of the whole, and none which would serve more effectually the part of a cobweb to hold fast for life the feeble flies which may be caught therein. To abandon a costume publicly adopted with high pretensions, would be an act of courage of which not many women perhaps are capable. Let it not be said that such distinction of dress is needful to allow ladies to pass safely through low districts for purposes of charity.

Our English populations (brutalized as, alas! they too often are) deserve not to be taunted with such obtuseness as to need a black robe and veil to make them recognise a woman to be respected. We happen to have intimately known a lady who for years together traversed, on her way to a ragged school, nearly alternate nights, in ordinary costume, one of the very worst districts of any city in England. Never once was she disturbed in any manner; nay, the poor creatures who often thronged the streets, in their wildest excitement made way civilly and silently for her to pass on her errand. The supposed imposing effect of monastic attire seems rather of a different nature, if we may credit Miss Goodman:—"On a wet day, when it was necessary to hold up the dress, our great enemies, the little boys, were in a state of considerable excitement."

Again, let us consider the two classes of nuns in every convent—the strong-willed and the weak. To the first, it is quite possible that a convent may prove to her a theatre whereon she may develop wonderful abilities for the government of the community and the direction of noble enterprises. In whatever line may lie the bent of her disposition, she may find a field wider than the private life of a woman can often supply, and female saints, from every point of the compass of asceticism or philanthropy, beckon her to follow their example, and rise to their glory. We have all heard somewhat of these powerful ladyabbesses, Anglican no less than Romanist. But is there no danger in all this—no peril that enthusiasm shall kindle into fanaticism—that fasts and vigils will result in spiritual delusions and spiritual pride, and that the government of a mother-superior shall degenerate into the tyranny of the hardest of despots? To stop in the career of enthusiasm at the moment when the feelings are beginning to lift us off the ground in their heated course, this is an act of self-control which assuredly needs no ordinary strength—strength of a kind rarest among woman's gifts. And to forbear to stretch guidance into government, and government into tyranny, is not this also a difficult task? Woman is assuredly not constituted to exercise outward legislative power. Her natural sphere of action is all inward. Even over children she best rules by winning, not by commanding. She loses somewhat of her womanhood when she subdues any one whatever by force of authority, and makes her will *dominate* theirs. She *can* do this. There are few women worth anything who cannot at sufficient call exercise that mysterious potency of volition which bears down before it the feeble wishes which are the substitutes for wills in weak natures. There is even perhaps something especially and portentously remarkable in the exertion of this moral force by one who is physically weak and delicate. A woman with a despotic, invasive will is quite a terrible being, before whom the gentle, the indolent, and the vacillating inevitably succumb. But such a woman is no true representative of her sex; her power is no more the true power of woman than a love-philtre's charm would be the same as the charm of beauty and goodness. Enough has been revealed to us of the secrets of convents, to leave no doubt that the possession of unnatural authority by the superiors has continually proved too strong a temptation; and the woman who in her natural domestic sphere might have been the gentlest of guides, has become in a convent the cruellest of petty despots.

For the woman of weaker fibre, who never attains to supremacy in her nunnery, what a crushing down of her whole nature must the system effect! To say that a woman accustomed to all the liberty of an English lady in our time, returns at thirty to her boarding-school, and remains there for the rest of her life in pupilage, is to give but a faint idea of the trammels of every convent life. The absence of the invigorating influence of freedom of movement—of intercourse with the sound strong minds of men—or even of women mixing freely in the world—the endless monotony of life causing each little daily molehill of annoyance to become a mountain when multiplied by all the days it has to be endured,—all these things must tend to make the mind weaker, and duller, and smaller every day. Perhaps the advocates of asceticism will tell us all such privations and annoyances are nothing when voluntarily incurred and endured *en esprit de penitence.* Fully, indeed, must we admit that under high religious excitement, not only such things as these, but positive sufferings, are either unfelt or transmuted into a superhuman pleasure. Like the beautiful old legend of Pisa, the saint hugs thorns to his breast and they become roses. And if any endurance whatever be really demanded of us by God, I cannot doubt that the grace to bear it is never taken away, but grows into that celestial peace we may see on the countenance of many a poor victim of agonizing disease or bereavement. But when the suffering is all voluntary and arbitrary, then we believe that, when the enthusiasm which prompted it has subsided with the inevitable ebb of all human feelings, then there is nothing to replace it, nothing to prevent the laws of our nature from asserting themselves, calling out for the natural food of the affections and the intellect, and growing starved and sick as it is denied.

There is but too much reason to fear, that on women of this class the effect of conventual discipline is to freeze even the spirit of charity itself into the hard character of a duty of routine. There is an ever-present danger in perfect *organization,* that it should degenerate into perfect *mechanism.* The nun who, under orders from her superior, goes the round of so many beds at stated hours, must in the long run find it hard not to perform her duty with the same sense of monotony as a housemaid who dusts so many chairs against a wall. Let her struggle as she will against weariness and the depression of servitude, nature will still in a degree assert itself. No one can retain the fresh feelings of free work followed intelligently and from spontaneous sympathy, with the constrained attitude of mechanical obedience. This is a hard saying, and we would not dwell on it too strongly in face of the evidence of the great and noble devotion of hundreds of Sisters of Charity in all parts of the world. We should not have mentioned it at all, but that our own experience in Italy and France, corroborated by the testimony of physicians of many nations, assured us that such dangers to the feebler sort of minds among nuns were by no means visionary. Happening to witness an instance of hardness and even cruelty shown to a dying woman in the hospital of St. Maria Nuova, at Florence, by a Sister of Charity, we have been led for some years to institute all the inquiry in our power, and the result is as we have stated. As it is for these feebler women especially that monastic direction claims to be so peculiarly useful, it is well that we should at the same time remember how much it is calculated to depress them into machines, the gain of whose outward service is more than counterbalanced by the loss of that genuine sympathy and tenderness, without which "to give our bodies to be burned profiteth nothing." Soldiers may possibly do their work very well as *fighting machines*, but a nun who becomes a *nursing machine* is worse than useless.

We shall not soon forget the impression made on us by the recital of a friend who was nursed through a fever in Paris by a Sister of Charity, who tended her much as an indolent groom might tend a horse. "Do you imagine," the Sister said to her one day, "that I serve you *for your sake?* No; I do it only *pour faire mon salut.*" For days and weeks of pain and helplessness she was obliged to receive every service rendered in this inhuman spirit. A warm-hearted and most loveable woman, she bore during her whole illness the presence of this devout automaton, feeling that even such ill-performed attentions as she received were all so many additions to the nun's spiritual capital earned out of her helplessness —a drink might be a day out of purgatory, the arrangement of her pillow a step towards Paradise. We hope that among Protestant orders no such spirit of what Coleridge called "other worldliness," such spiritual selfishness, would ever be authorized. But we rather "hope" so than feel any great security in the matter.

We have left ourselves no space to speak of the proposal which has been made as an amendment to that of sisterhoods—namely, that of the establishment of *deaconesses* in England. Some of the arguments in the preceding pages will apply to the case, others will pass it by. On the whole, perhaps it may be looked on as a suggestion of greater value than the other, yet fraught with its own special difficulties. Let the Church of England be given never so high an estimate, and its clergy credited with never so great prudence, the relation of such a female order as that of deaconesses to the Church, and of such an individual as a deaconess to a parochial clergyman, is not exempt from difficulties and objections. Grievous would it be if the field of philanthropic labour were to be made the arena of sectarian strife or of petty local jealousies and cabals. Will the world have no patience to try the association principle a little longer? Must steam give way to stage-coaches, or stage-coaches to the still earlier good practice of the horseman with a lady *on a pillion?*

In conclusion, we earnestly commend to those who seek the re-establishment of monasticism in England, the careful and solemn consideration of the dangers which such a scheme involves. We do not affirm that these dangers may not be averted. It may be possible to build our new institutes of charity upon the very ground for ages filled with the malaria of asceticism, and yet so perfectly to thorough-drain it as that no taint of the old poison may remain. It *may* be possible, albeit a dangerous experiment; but if there is to be any hope of success, the whole peril must be understood on all hands, and the future Anglican Sisters of Charity must enter their vocation with a full comprehension that their purpose is different, and that their motives and principles must be different, from those of their predecessors. They must bear in mind that their object is not *to earn salvation for themselves* by penitential practices and meritorious "works," but *to do good to others;* that the poor may be more effectually relieved, the sick better nursed, the sinful better reclaimed. They must bear in mind that instead of enfeebling their bodies by fasting and watching, and thus (as old Zoroaster well said) "sinfully weakening the powers entrusted to them for good," they are bound more than any other women to hoard the life and strength they have devoted to their fellow-creatures. They must bear in mind that despotic power and blind obedience are both of them in their nature immoral, and that no vow can be justified or binding which, in matters of conscience, would control the actions of a rational free agent. And, lastly, they must bear in mind that although charity is a holy and noble cause for devotion, it is not exclusively or super-eminently sacred, but that the natural duties of life are before all voluntary dedications; that the names of mother, daughter, wife, are holier than that of nun; and that all faithful work—be it in the fields of art and science, or disinterested labour of any kind—is as truly *work for God,* as the toil of the most devoted of philanthropists.

# ESSAY V.

## WOMEN IN ITALY, IN 1862.

*Reprinted from Macmillan's Magazine for September*, 1862.

It has become almost a truism to observe that the progress of a nation in civilization must, in a considerable measure, depend on the condition of its women. At the present moment, therefore, when universal attention is directed towards Italy, as the regenerated land arising to take once more its place among the kingdoms of the earth, it becomes a matter of interest to observe the position held by Italian Women, and the promises held out of the performance on their part of their proper share in the work of national restoration. In venturing to throw together a few facts and reflections on this subject, I must deprecate all claim to an adequate treatment of it; which would demand far greater experience than that afforded me by four limited periods of residence in different parts of Italy.

The social relations between English and Italian ladies are usually so slight, and our connexion with the humbler classes so limited and transitory, that, at the best of times, our impressions are liable to be extremely erroneous, and we are bound to put them forward with diffidence. Nothing seems harder than to attain a comprehension of the *inner* life of our fellow-creatures who have passed their years in an atmosphere morally and mentally different from our own; and, in failing to appreciate this inner life, we necessarily fall into a thousand errors as regards the *outer* manners; and misinterpret the few facts presented to us. We have many of us enjoyed a good laugh at the pictures of England drawn by Frenchmen—the accounts of the *grandes dames* who always have their carafes at dinner filled with gin instead of water; the never-forgotten nobleman who, in every novel, sells his wife with a rope round her neck; *Sir Smith,* who is always eating raw steaks and assaulting *les policemen;* the celebrated *Cottage dans Belgrave Squar,* described in "*Les mystères de Londres,*" as visited by *Lord Dogge;* and the *Office appointed by the Church of England for the Exorcism of Ghosts,* quoted authoritatively by Dumas, in "*Le Pasteur d'Ashbourne.*" With these warnings before our eyes, it behoves us to talk with some reservation about the manners and customs of other nations.

A very obvious and unmistakable distinction, however, is that which exists between the people of

Northern and Southern Italy, as regards their consideration for women as well as in so many other respects. Descending from the Alps we pass through populations more or less inheritors of that Teutonic blood in which a respect for females has existed from the earliest ages; and here, accordingly, we find the Sardinians, the "English of Italy," aiming at a real education for their daughters, and boasting, among their matrons, of ladies who have taken no small part in the social improvements of their country. Further on, we have the Tuscans, whose exquisite courtesy and gentleness of nature could hardly fail to display itself in their treatment of woman, whatever might be her personal claims to respect. But, as we go further south, through Rome to Naples, we seem to pass through a constantly descending scale, till, in the latter city, we arrive at a condition of degradation painful to witness. The most transient visitor can hardly fail to be struck with the alternation of brutal roughness, and still more insufferable familiarity, with which any lady, who ventures out alone, however closely veiled, is sure to be treated; and a longer experience tends to display more than a mere departure from good manners. An English lady, long resident at Naples, and married to a Neapolitan, informed me that, till of late years, it was customary among the poorer classes to hang a small black flag out of the window of the apartment wherein a girl was born, to save the painful necessity of informing inquirers of the unfortunate sex of the infant. She, herself, after having given birth to her third child, the two eldest being boys, was much alarmed at finding both her doctor and nurse remaining silent. Naturally she feared some disaster, and, on her urgent intreaties, they at last broke to her the terrible information that she was the mother of a very fine little girl!

These differences between the south and the north (taking Italy as a whole)—between Italian women and those of trans-Alpine countries—arise doubtless from causes too deep to be here investigated. The popular opinion, that it is to any special form of religion that woman owes the elevation she holds among us, seems refuted by the most cursory observation. Christianity, while raising generally the moral standard of mankind, and impressing on all the value of human souls, has, of course, done much in a broad way towards abolishing old despotisms, both of class, race, and sex. But the fact remains, that the woman of the north, who was free and honoured in the heathen days of Tacitus, is free and honoured now; and the woman of the south, who was looked down on by heathen Greeks, Syrians, and Romans, is not one whit less looked down on by their Christian descendants. Indeed, it may be doubted whether any modern southern race entertains even such share of honour for women as the Romans and Spartans accorded to their matrons; and among the Levantine Christians (as I was myself informed in Cairo, by one most competent to judge, the French Superior of the Convent and School of *Le Bon Pasteur*), the condition of their women is quite as degraded as that of the women among their Moslem neighbours. Cause and effect are here so interwoven that it is almost idle to name, as the source of the evil, either the prevailing character of the women, or the treatment which, in the lapse of ages, has stamped that character almost ineffaceably. Yes; one fact is obvious. Wherever the higher nature in woman is preponderant over the lower, and she has more of the intellectual than the sensual, more of feeling than of passion, more of duty than of impulse, there she will be free and honoured. And, on the other hand, where all this is reversed, no arbitrary legislation, no intervention of even a Mariolatrous Church, can exalt her above the condition of a toy and a slave.

The various classes of society are marked in Italy by sharper lines of division than amongst us now in England, and, in fact, almost as clearly as in France under the *ancien régime*. Between the nobles and the "*mezzo cetto*" order there is a gulf which the boldest adventurers on either side rarely venture to pass, so far as to engage in the social relations of visits and assemblies; and when, by any chance, the most learned and cultivated physician, or the most charming wife of a judge, finds him or herself in an evening party of ducas and marchesas, it is much as easy and agreeable to all parties as if an English squire were to invite his blacksmith's family to take tea in his drawing-room. In considering the condition of Italian women, it is thus obviously needful to distinguish always the social ranks of those of whom we may be speaking. The habits, education, and ideas of the one are by no means those of the other.

An Italian lady of rank received always, till lately, her education at a convent. In Rome, that of the Trinità was the fashionable boarding-school for the whole order. Of late years, however, among the very highest families, it has become customary to keep the daughters of the house at home, and to give them, under a suitable governess, the instruction of masters, for languages, music, &c. Much desire seems to exist to make this instruction as complete as possible. French and English are almost universally learned, and a small share of geography and history. Thus it is not the fault of the parents if their daughters remain with an education after all of a very limited kind. It is the misfortune of the whole Italian nation, whose own literature is as yet unawakened from the torpor of ages, and who are (so long as they are obedient to priestly authority) debarred from access to all the living literature of the world. To be well read in Italian literature is (for these young ladies) to have read Dante, and Tasso, and some *very* choice excerpts of Ariosto and Boccaccio, together with, among modern books, a little of Silvio Pellico, a little of

Alfieri, and those eternal dull novels *Le Promessi Sposi*, *Le Fidanzate Ligure*, *Sibylla*, *Odaleta*, and *Ettore Fieramosca.* Beyond these there is always some reason, political, religious, or prudish, why they are to wade no further in the rather shallow waters of later Italian literature. Then, as to foreign books, French novels are of course under a justifiable embargo (for the higher classes only, however), and French science, history, and philosophy are all condemned for other reasons as unsound and dangerous. Of German, Greek, or Latin, nothing is known. Remains then only English literature; and assuredly nothing better could be desired *if* they were only free to profit by its resources. But to teach the English language to a young lady who is bound by the rules of the *Index Expurgatorius*, and the still stricter regulations of her confessor and her governess is pretty much like Bluebeard giving his wife the key of the red chamber, and telling her at the same time never to open it, for if she do so it will be her destruction. It is downright mockery to bestow the glorious tongue of Shakespeare and Milton, Hooker and Taylor, Locke and Hamilton, Gibbon and Macaulay, Shelley and Tennyson, and then say, "Not one of these great writers must yon ever read; but go and find in a few second-rate novels and tour-books—a dozen volumes out of the *Tauchnitz Collection*—your reward for acquiring the most difficult of modern languages."

It is a fact which will doubless call forth a laugh,

but which is in truth deplorable enough, that, a short time ago, the education of a daughter of one of the noblest families in Rome having been completed on the above system, it was decided that, before marrying and entering society, it was desirable that she should have read *one* book of the class of which foreigners are in the habit of talking at evening parties! Serious consultations on the important topic of what this book should be, ended in the selection of "Uncle Tom's Cabin," as the work which, on the whole, would form the best basis for general conversation. But was the princess to read Mrs. Stowe's story, with all its heretical theology, *pur et simple?* Such a thing could not be thought of. A digest was compiled by the confessor—a pretty little abridgment of the tale, in about fifty or sixty pages of manuscript; and this safe and wholesome extract, divested of all the poisonous ingredients of the original beverage, was duly administered to the youthful lips. Armed, at last, with so large an acquisition, in the way of modern literature, the princess boldly descended into the arena of balls and receptions, and asked everybody she met, "Had they read that charming new book, *Lo Zio Tom?*"

Such is the ordinary education of the noble ladies of Rome. There exists, however, among them one single exception—a Phœnix, a Vittoria Colonna, a "regular blue,"—regarded by all with awe and astonishment. This lady, the Marchesa B——à, habitually reads the best French and English books as they appear, *so far as they can be obtained in Rome,* (which is very little indeed). The surprise created by accomplishments and habits shared by every cultivated woman in our country seems to afford a very just measure of the rarity of them among the ladies of Italy.

In all classes, and among both sexes, there exists in Italy, as in all Catholic countries, a want whose magnitude we are apt to calculate solely on its theological side, to the oblivion of its general educational bearings. In England and Scotland, every man, woman, and child, who can read at all, has read more or less of the greatest book of the world. The whole literature of the most religious and deep-hearted race of antiquity, of the most sublimely poetic of Eastern nations, lies between the brown lids of the little familiar Bibles each Sunday-school child manages to buy for himself with a few hoarded sixpences; and, however serious may be the mistakes popularly connected with it, as regards theology, the result as regards the intellectual life and poetic feelings of the whole mass of our nation is, doubtless, beneficial beyond estimation. Suppose that the Bible were taken out of England, and theology taught solely as in Italy by the clergy, *vivâ voce,* and in catechisms and wretched compendiums in modern phraseology. Can we imagine the tomes of Eastern and Western classics, which would suffice in any way to replace it as a vehicle of popular instruction? A people whose mental food for ages has been such meat and wine as Job, and the Psalms, and the Parables, and the Pauline Epistles, must needs be in a very different state of constitution from one which has fed on the poor milk and water of miraculous legends of the Madonna, and Lives of the Saints, and all the spiritual pap and sugar-candy of Romanism.

Again. Both men and women in Italy are inconceivably depressed in mental rank by the embargo which has lain for ages on all social discussions of either religion or politics. It is actually a precept of the Church, that matters of theology and divinity ought never to be talked of between laymen. As a priest, preaching this very winter in Rome, explained it, "We of the clergy have spent years in such studies, under the best instruction, and yet we can hardly venture to speak about them, from the imminent danger of expressing ourselves in some heterodox manner on one point or another. How, then, is it to be permitted that unlearned laymen, or, above all things, that *women* should dare to open their mouths on religious subjects?" All that immense range of topics, then, which pertains to our relation to God or conception of His nature, our deepest feelings in this world, and our hopes hereafter, are "barred and banned, forbidden fare" to the Italian. If we could imagine such a precept thoroughly carried out, the result would be the most deplorable thing in the world. I cannot believe that it is so in truth; but yet it is certain that habitual silence on matters of religion is cultivated, and that the priest alone is instructor and confidant. Doubtless the marked *objectivity* of the Italian character, the absence of reflection and self-consciousness, renders it easier for them than it would be for a northern race to obey this sacerdotal order of silence. Even the good ones among them probably *think* little even if they *feel* much. But yet some expansion of heart must often be needed, and then how inexpressibly injurious must be a principle which, in the name of religion, would close their lips to the expression of religious thought! The fire may kindle, but it is a sin to speak with the tongue. Thus, then, a man may rightly admire the wonders of creation, may cast his eyes over all this glorious beauty of Italian earth, and seas, and skies; but when the thought comes to him of the God who made it, he must not turn to wife or friend and speak of that God. He may rightly addict himself to natural science and pursue the chain as far as he may through its lower links, but never may he trace it upward, and bind it to the eternal throne. In other words, he may speak of *facts;* but on all which raises facts into *truths*, which gives them their background of meaning, which makes the heavens declare the glory of God, and the whole earth show His praise, he must for ever be silent. Husband and wife, mother and child, sister and sister, may go through life's dark places side by side, but never may they talk by the way of Him who is guiding them.

Never, in the overflowings of joy, may they speak of their loving Father freely, with the confidence of His happy children. The struggles of penitence, of aspiration, of anxious doubt, and trembling faith—all these are hidden for ever from the eyes which look on them with that human love which is the ray to tell us of the brightness of the love Divine. No wonder, then, is it, that while all the deep channels of spiritual sympathy are closed, and the words which might convey it whispered only in the dull ear of a confessor, no wonder is it if the ties of natural affections be slackened, if family relations lose their sanctity amid the struggles of life, and finally fail altogether in the last supreme moment, and the poor dying husband, wife, parent, brother, child, is left to pass away with no ministrations save those of the priest, no loving breast on which to rest the drooping head, no gentle hand to wipe the death-dew from the brow, no beloved voice to whisper of God's strength in our weakness, no

> "Tender farewell on the shore
> Of this rude world."

Never, I believe, would Italians desert the dying (as they habitually do, even where there is no possibility of contagion), if religious sympathies were permitted to be to them what they are to us—the undertone of the harmony of this life, and the prophecy of an immortal friendship in the world of souls. The priest has come in, thrusting himself between every relation, between husband and wife, between mother and child, between each soul and its Father in heaven. It is not the husband who leads the prayers of his family; it is not the mother who teaches her daughter the lessons of faith and love; it is not the friend who "takes sweet counsel" on sacred things—but always the priest, always the priest! No marvel, then, is it, that, at the last awful hour, the cord of human love, unstrengthened by its golden strand of holiest sympathies, snaps rudely in twain, and to the priest it is left to stand alone by the dying bed, and touch with *olio santo* the stiffening limbs, and read his Latin invocations, which the dull ear of the death-stricken never so much as hears, and which seem rather to be incantations to unseen powers of evil than prayers to the everlasting Father who is opening wide His arms to bring home the soul of His child.

It is not only, however, the eternal interests of religion which are forbidden themes of intercourse among the people of Italy. Till the new order of things, it was everywhere throughout the Peninsula a matter of extremest peril to discuss political questions of any kind, even in the strictest private circles. No one could tell where the spy or the traitor might lurk; and dungeons—Austrian, Papal, or Neapolitan—were not to be trifled with for the sake of mere conversation. Of course, all this holds good as much as ever in Rome and Venice to this day, *among the Italians themselves.* It is not to be forgotten by English visitors, that the liberty of tongue and pen *they* can securely exercise would insure the destruction of the unhappy subjects of these paternal Governments.

Now, it may seem a small matter (especially for women) to be debarred from talking politics. Many a frivolous Englishwoman would, perhaps, hail it as almost a boon if she were never to hear any more of elections, and bills, and ministries, or of the Essays and Reviews, and Biblical Interpretation, and Darwin's Hypothesis. But the truth is, that conversation, without freedom to rise into serious discussion, is no true conversation at all, but mere wretched tittle-tattle, gossip, and froth. It is not that any of us want to discuss religion and politics all day long; but we all of us feel that it is, at any moment, at our option to pursue the subject of the moment into those deeper questions which lie at its root—to open up any one channel of human thought which may suggest itself. Thus, the tendency of our conversation, as years go on, and education and science are widening, and individualism asserting itself more freely, is constantly to become of a more intellectual and solid character. A "good talk" among a party of cultivated English or Americans is a really good thing; and if it want some of the artificial polish, the finesse and epigram, of the old school of the Hotel Rambouillet, it doubtless more than attains a counterbalance by its spontaneity and simplicity, its force and earnestness. A process absolutely the reverse of this has been going on in Italy for centuries, up to the last few years of hope and regeneration. When all deep subjects are forbidden, the tendency of conversation is ever to keep further and further away from them, and to evade the awkwardness and peril of an approach which must needs be fatal to anything like earnestness. Accordingly, a light and graceful description of last night's opera, a critique on the toilette of the ladies in company, a dissertation on the equipages of the afternoon in the Corso, the Chiaja, or the Cascine, and a serious argument concerning the latest scandal of the society, pretty well exhaust the resources of Italian conversation. The heads of the talkers might be fairly likened to children's balloon toys, seeming to struggle which is lightest, till all are found bobbing against the ceiling together.

In other matters also, beside literary pleasures and intellectual conversation, the lives of Italian ladies are sadly limited. Except for the short summer *villeggiatura*, they have no habits of country life, nor of the duties which thence arise so naturally and blessedly among the wives and daughters of our landed proprietors, of attending to the wants of their dependants. Neither do Italian ladies, while residing in their town houses, often concern themselves with visiting the neighbouring poor, or the sick in the hospitals. On this subject I have endeavoured to obtain all the information possible, both in the institutions themselves and among the Italian ladies. From all I can learn, the most active and useful of the lay philanthropists of Italy, south of Genoa, are not Italians at all, but foreigners. The fame of the English princesses, Borghese and Doria, is European; but besides these I everywhere hear of Russians and Poles as interesting themselves in schools and in the out-of-door sick paupers. One of these, who died lately in Rome, the Princess Volkonsky, lived in the most abject want that she might educate and support thirty-five poor girls in her palace. Another Russian countess is still grievously lamented by all the poor. "Ah, Signora, her stairs were crowded all day, and she helped us all." In Florence, the Marchesa S——, born a Russian princess, kindly volunteered to show me the admirable infant and poor school under her patronage, (partly supported by Prince D——, another Russian).* Several American ladies resident in Rome also employ themselves constantly in visiting the sick poor. In the huge hospitals of San Spirito, San Giovanni, and Santa Maria Nuova (of Florence), I was unable to hear that any lay ladies ever visited, the charge of the sick being wholly in the hands of French and Italian nuns of various orders. In the Female Reformatory and Gaol of the Termini it is the same; Belgian sisters manage everything, and have no visitors. Only at the terrible hospital of San Giacomo, which

* Since writing the above I have been informed, on the best authority, that many Florentine ladies are now interesting themselves in philanthropic labours of various kinds; foremost among them is the gifted Marchesa D., who paints pictures for the support of her schools.

receives the most disgusting diseases, and which even a well-accustomed head can hardly endure for unutterable noisomeness, did I come on the traces of lay Italian visitors. The nun of San Luigi, who accompanied me, told me that once a month, ladies, including some countesses whom she greatly revered, paid visits regularly. "What did they do for the patients?" I inquired. I confess I was not a little astounded by the reply, that the principal thing they did was to *comb their hair!* The Italian ladies are assuredly far too kind-hearted to let their intercourse stop at this senseless service—which, of course, was the proper task of the numerous paid nurses, or house-servants, who work under the nuns. Still it gave me a shock to find this new trace of the great moral plague of Catholicism—the treating charity as a matter of spiritual earning to the giver, rather than of natural benefit to the receiver. It is like the monster farce of the washing of the pilgrims' feet at Easter. The good of the *object* of charity is the last thing considered, but as an act of humility and self-denial it is believed to purchase no small heavenly gain for the *agent.* There is assuredly something peculiarly revolting in this idea of making spiritual capital for ourselves out of the miseries of our fellows, and that, too, by performing acts ostentatiously serviceable, although really mere mockeries of their wants. The poor wretches in the female wards of San Giacomo present, I may safely affirm, one of the most awful sights on earth. Two enormous halls open right and left, crowded respectively with the victims of the most agonizing and the most revolting of human diseases. The hall to the left is appropriated to cancer and other "*plagi*" of hideous cutaneous disorders. The beds are arranged closely in quadruple rows, the head of one patient touching the feet of another—in all 130 patients. Everywhere there is dirt, disorder, and noisomeness unutterable. As I walked up and down again, through the central passage between the beds, all the hapless creatures started up and joined in one piteous yell for alms, stretching their hands as if to seize me, and displaying with eager haste every loathsome horror of their sufferings. It was truly like a vision of Dante, where all the lost souls in the pit are grasping at his cloak to hold him back. To be told that ladies visited these hapless creatures was a great relief. But what did they do for their succour? "*They combed their hair!*" It seemed nothing more nor less than wanton mockery.

There is no workhouse, properly speaking, in Rome, and there is an immense amount of poverty and wretchedness outside the hospitals. Except, however, for the few American and Russian ladies of whom I have spoken, I have failed to hear of any visitors to the poor. All is left to the nuns. And here we see one of the endless evils of Monachism. It separates the duty of charity from domestic duty, making the one the task of the nun alone, and the other of the wife and mother. Thus all healthful alternation is prevented. The woman who is living in the warm atmosphere of natural affections may not carry out from thence the blessings of a softened heart; neither may she carry back into her home that blessed glow of spirit, and bracing of the soul to duty, which follows all real work among the poor. Let it be admitted that the heavier part of all such labours must be done by single women, and that it is much to be desired that Protestant unmarried ladies took it as universally as their proper vocation as do Romanists. Still, that they should be *free*—should remain essentially lay members of society, taking their place in family and social circles, and co-operating with married women, their sisters, mothers, daughters, as these have time and power to aid them—this is absolutely needful, I believe, to make society what it ought to be, and to prevent the consecration of the cloister from being the desecration of the home.

I have sometimes thought I could read the results of the narrow moral and intellectual life of the women of Italy in the aspect of their faces and manner of deportment. There is much beauty among them, and usually a look of quick and vivid intelligence; but there is a most painful blank beside. If I might be guilty of a bull, I should almost call it a *conscious blank*. They seem made for something better; but yet one can read on brow, or eyes, or mouth, no trace of thoughts beyond an opera, or a new bonnet, or some petty quarrel of social jealousy. As I have confessed, I have really seen too little of Italy in only four visits to offer a reliable opinion. I can but give my own impression, always renewed; and that is as I have said. The faces of women of the working classes seem much like those of their order elsewhere, bearing the traces, alas! of toil and hard sharp cares; but not morally unhealthy in aspect. But the great ladies in their splendid *toilettes* seem to bear on their faces that curse—far surpassing all "Curse of Labour"—the Curse of Idleness—of emptiness of brain, or inanition of the pulses, which constitute the true life of a human being as distinguished from a doll to be dressed or a child to be amused. Weariness, vacancy, trivial pleasure, or petty annoyance, these are the common expressions; and yet through all a certain anxiety, a sort of hunger after something better and nobler. Truly, if I have read them rightly, a pitiable story! If one of them could understand her own lot, and compare it with that of her free and happy sister in our dull Isle of Fogs, of which they have such dread, how sad, how unendurable would it seem! In girlhood she has had none of our free country habits of healthy rides and romps in the hay, and winter evening games. She has been kept from all intercourse, save a very formal one, under strictest *surveillance,* even with the young ladies of her own rank. As she grows older, she has no free walks, no delicious storybooks, no hoarded poems to feed with pure fire the kindling spirits of youth, the dawning love for the beautiful, the sublime, the heroic. And then, while yet a mere girl, all immature in heart and mind, she is married, if not *against* her wish, yet with her private feelings having, probably, been the last item in the requirements of her parents when they accepted the proposals of a man who has hardly twice seen her —who has certainly never conversed with her for an hour, inasmuch as *till* thus engaged she can never appear in society. Of the result of such *mariages de convenance* in Italy, it is hard to speak. Probably, there is some difference in different parts of the country. In Naples it is universally declared to be an atrocious immorality. Rome, always full of prudery, claims especially domestic morality for its great nobility. It is at all events the fashion among them for the idle husband to dangle constantly beside his idle wife; and, if wrong exist, it is carefully hidden from public sight. If free from offence, however, these lives of the great Roman nobility are at best useless and inane beyond all conception. A country where a noble layman has no political career, no office in the state or army which he can condescend to fulfil (except walking in processions in the *Guardia Nobile*), a country where there is no literature worth naming, no newspapers worth reading, no field sports, no benches of country magistrates, no parliament, no committees, no elections of any kind—in such a country the life of a man of rank is a poor thing indeed. A few of them have tried to occupy themselves with obtaining fine breeds of horses and cattle; and they all act as their own agents and auditors of accounts, expressing astonishment at English noblemen who trust anybody with implicit confidence in such matters. But beyond these employments there is actually little or nothing for them to do. The powerful and factious nobles of old, with their strange lives of violence and crime gilded over like that of Nero by dilettantism in Art—the Orsini, Colonnas, and Borgias of old—have given place to a race who pick cautiously their steps along the very narrowest path of existence possible for a human being; who spend their mornings over their account-books, their afternoons in a drive with their wives up and down the Corso and the Pincian, and their evenings at cards for a paul a game with their uncle, the cardinal. When they die, their epitaphs mention most truly, among the foremost of their virtues, that they were "Prudent and Frugal;" Such a prince, duke, or marquis, for a husband, will hardly raise a woman's nature to any very lofty altitudes of feeling.

Let us now try to obtain a glimpse of the condition of the women of the *mezzo cetto* class—a class extending, with only trifling shades of social rank, from the wives and daughters of professional men down to keepers of small shops, dressmakers, &c. In the first place, their domestic life is not what we call "comfortable." That truly English word, as Hawthorne says, has no application whatever to the apartments of a great rambling Italian palace, in which each family has its half-dozen rooms, with kitchen and scullery all on the same floor, and a great staircase (cold, dark, and dirty, nine times out of ten), to share with five or six other families. Every Italian woman is so far a Psyche that she always comes out in butterfly guise on Sundays, and Festas, and fine afternoons; but the rest of her days, and in the "bosom of her family," her state, alas! is very much that of the same butterfly in its grub condition. Such alternations of dirt and splendour are happily confined with us to our cooks and housemaids. Neither has the Italian much excuse, as regards household labours, for her matutinal dishabille and violation of the sacro-sanct institution of the morning bath. A room cleaned as an English housewife would clean it is a thing I can safely affirm I have never beheld in Italy. The frescoed ceilings and cornices, the ill-painted, ill-jointed woodwork, the large immovable and yet ricketty couches, ready to break to pieces if shoved a step on the carpets which are nailed down for the season over a bed of musty straw—it were utterly futile to expect such apartments and such furniture to be what we call clean. Then, as to cookery. The whole Italian nation possesses that quality which some would term a virtue, but which is in truth always a misfortune to the race which inherits it—an indifference to all varieties and luxuries of food. Like the poor Irish, contented for ever with their potatoes and stirabout, there is wanted a stimulus for wifely cares wherever both parties are satisfied without the woman's exertion of a little thought and skill, and the whole domestic life loses somewhat thereby. In Italy, for foreigners, there is the eternal *trattoria* tin-box, out of which the unwholesome dinner is taken, ready served in dishes, at the proper hour. For natives, there is the undressed salad and the sour bread, and the *minestra* and *lesso* (the soup and boiled-down meat), and very little beside, unless *fritta,* a hotchpot of fish, poultry, or vegetables, fried in oil. English crockery and English cutlery must be used even by the poor, and, of course, are used very sparingly. Their own hideous delf (as an Italian lady said to me) "breaks if you only look at it." Of course, many ablutions of the same, knife-boards, and the like, are very slightly in request. Washing, however, does go on—washing of clothes. Every day, everywhere, may be seen on the lines, hung like cobwebs across every court and angle, and on the long canes stuck out of windows of palaces, arrays of garments dangling in the breeze. I am at this moment writing opposite a large and handsome building—a public college, founded by one pope, restored by another. At its windows, opening on one of the best streets of Rome, there are fixed *en permanence* strings and canes for drying clothes; and for half the week the stone *façade* of the college is pleasingly diversified by rows of pupil's stockings, shirts, &c.,

and, now and then, a few pairs of sheets. Nobody dreams there is any indecency in this, or in a hundred other things in Rome, which would shock us not a little in England.

Light as it is, and imperfectly accomplished at the best, the Italian lady of the *mezzo cetto* never dreams of training her servant to fulfil her domestic task by herself. She spends her own time half-helping, half-scolding, half-gossiping with her maids, backwards and forwards between the beds which they are making, the dinner they are cooking, and that lounge to which the whole nation betakes itself at every spare moment —the window. *Walking* in the street must never be done alone; but out of her window at the 1st, 2d, 3d, or *ultimo piano* she may lean and gaze for hours on the most public thoroughfare, and, moreover, smile and exchange words with the passengers, in all propriety. Of this liberty every one avails herself in full, wasting whole hours staring up and down and interchanging comments with her *donna di servizia* (maid of all work), or *cameriera* (lady's maid), as the case may be, in the adjoining window. I have often laughed to watch the rows of heads to be seen in profile all down the different stories of windows in a very dull street on an ordinary day when there was actually nothing to see beyond a man with a cart of oranges, a hack carriage or two, and a little *lupetta* dog poking his sharp nose among the cabbage stalks and other filth in the *Immondezzaio,* which (of course) adorned the corner in perpetuity, having its name printed on the house over it for fear of any mistake.

This is the morning life of an Italian, beginning rather early and ending at two or three o'clock in winter, and quite late in the cool of the evening in summer. There is actually very little else done; very little music or needlework, or teaching of children; and actually *no* reading in nine cases out of ten. Few Italian ladies' drawing-rooms ever show a single book, paper, or pamphlet of any kind, but only rubbishy ornaments of glass, artificial flowers in gaudy French china vases; or, perhaps, some natural flowers carefully mounted on wires by the dealer, and set up in that formal manner, as unlike a real bouquet freshly arranged by an English lady's hands, as the dead Capuchins in the shrouds are unlike living men. When Italian women—who are not of the class carefully guarded from all but expurgated editions of "Uncle Tom's Cabin"—attempt to read at all, their studies invariably tend towards French novels or translations of them into Italian. The coarsely vicious "Dame aux Camellias" seems to be the chief favourite. I have been amazed to hear nicely-mannered young women, in the shops where I have managed to fall into conversation, quietly cite this as the book they liked best. Then came all Dumas's follies. If there were anything better to counterpoise such a literature it would be of small consequence; but there is actually nothing. All knowledge of life and morals must come through this distorted and polluted channel. To these books, apparently, the priests make small objection among the poorer women. An Italian servant told me that her cousin had had a Bible, and "oh, it was a beautiful book! But a priest saw it one day, and was very angry, and took it away." They take the Bible, but leave the "Dame aux Camellias."

The afternoon or evening having arrived, Psyche emerges; after a very long sojourn at her toilet—the grub has become a most radiant butterfly. Over an enormous crinoline falls a rich silk petticoat, sweeping at every step the dirty streets of Rome; a most elegant *chapeau de Paris* set on the fine head, with the hair *à l'Imperatrice;* a mantle, in winter of velvet; in summer of lace. I am not talking of princesses or marchesas. This is the toilet of people who keep small shops, and of the wives and daughters of *employés* of the middle and humbler grades. How and where the money comes from for this senseless dress is a question not to be discussed in this place. One thing is certain; all family comfort, and even proper food and fuel, is sacrificed unhesitatingly by all classes to these matters of display—to dress, to a box at the theatre, and to a carriage for a drive on the Pincian or in the Villa Borghese.

Respecting the humblest class of Italian women I have not much to say. They are not especially badly off in Florence and Rome. Female labour is well paid, comparatively to the price of the necessaries of life and the value of mens' labour. A *donna di facienda* (charwoman) earns 3 pauls (1*s.* 3*d.*) a day. A work-girl, 3 or 4 pauls and two meals. Slop-workers at their own homes earn from 5 to 8 pauls, and if they can do the more difficult parts of tailoring, such as the button-holes, they can readily earn a scudo (4*s.* 2*d.*) a day. With their habits this is absolute wealth, and the work-women themselves spoke of it to me as an excellent trade. As servants, all Italians are exceedingly good-humoured, never seeming to care how much trouble they take, or to what jobs they are set. They are disorderly, untidy, and sometimes violently passionate, making the absurdest scenes with their Italian mistresses, who will permit it, and who fly into a rage in return, and then make it up afterwards. To others they are very respectful, with a gentle and *well-bred* courtesy far removed from obsequiousness, and exceedingly pleasing. English people sometimes talk of their dishonesty, but my experience goes to prove that they are remarkably trustworthy; their pilferings, if such there be, being very trifling indeed, and all valuables being quite safe in their hands. Their moderation and sobriety are really great; such faults and vices as they have lie in another direction. It is almost useless to say they do not speak truth, or, as I have heard it euphuistically expressed, "they always, on principle, postpone the interests of veracity to the purposes of the moment!" In this respect they are no worse and no better than

French, Swiss, or Irish servants; and, like the latter, their quick imaginations supply them with an inexhaustible supply of *myths*, perfectly astounding to the Anglo-Saxon's dull powers of invention. Whatever Romanists may allege, it is a fact, patent to the most casual observer, that truth, *as a virtue in itself*, is barely recognised at all by Catholic nations. They are charitable and kind, and perfectly ready to recognise that "to bear false witness AGAINST our neighbour" is a sin; but to "bear false witness" IN HIS FAVOUR is a totally different matter. On the contrary, such an act is, as the French say, *un mensonge sublime!* I recollect a poor Irishwoman once affording an amusing example of the utter inability under which she laboured to comprehend the nature of veracity. She appealed to a lady thus pathetically, "Ah, ma'am, won't you speak to the master for me? He says he doesn't believe me; and now, to show you I would not deceive his honour, I'll tell you the truth. He asked me, last week, how I was? and I told him I was finely, *though I was ready to drop!*" Could any English mind have conceived such a testimony to reliability!

Doubtless, false teaching has a terrible share in this evil, as well as the difference which should never be forgotten of imaginative and unimaginative races. In the land of Machiavelli, there has not existed for ages any sense of disgrace attaching to cunning fraud and deception, *in themselves*, but rather the contrary, as

Mr. Trollope has so amply shown in his life of Filippo Strozzi. Praise has been constantly lavished on the "*prudence*" of actions for which an English gentleman would be kicked out of every club in London. Then there is the religious teaching which ought to correct this low standard of public opinion, but which, to all human appearance, never does anything of the kind. An American lady here, becoming much attached to her Roman *cameriera*, endeavoured, for a long time to awaken her conscience to the sin of lying, and at last had reason to hope that she had succeeded in doing so. One day the woman returned from confession in a rather triumphant state of mind, and told her mistress, "that she was all wrong to have frightened her so much about her falsehoods. The priest had assured her that, if they were not '*giurate*' (sworn) lies, they were of no consequence—very small sins indeed."

The pleasantest part to think of in these poor souls' lives, is their innocent enjoyment of their holidays. I have often watched parties of them on a Sunday afternoon going out for their walk, the whole family together in brightest array, and with their black eyes dancing with animation, and the white teeth gleaming at every smile. A Roman Sunday seems to me the best thing about Rome. The shops are not open as in Paris, there is no actual business going on—only a few stalls and *cafés*, and the like, where there is no disorder and no intoxication. But the whole population takes holiday nevertheless. They come home early from church, eat their frugal dinners, and then, in their best clothes, start off all together, having locked up their apartments and put the key in their pockets. Up and down the streets they walk, talking to their friends—up the steps of the Trinità, and round the beautiful Pincian Hill, thronged with carriages, and musical with military bands playing in the midst of a handsome garden; then out by the Porta del Popolo, for a longer walk through the grand avenues and grassy glades of the Villa Borghese; and home at last, at nightfall, through the Corso, talking and smiling as gaily and yet as soberly as when they started, till they climb up to their proper landing and open their door, and sit down to supper, having brought home a store of health and pleasure for the week to come.

In concluding this brief sketch of Italian women, in 1862, I cannot but feel that it is, on the whole, a sad and unhopeful one. The country which once produced Cornelias and Lucretias, and again, after two thousand years, gloried in the constellation of gifted women, of whom Vittoria Colonna and Olympia Morata were the types—that country *ought* surely, even yet, to possess daughters capable of aiding her uprise out of the night of superstition and despotism. It may be so; such Italian women may exist, and may start forth any day from their obscurity; but as yet we see them not. As in the loveliest of Rome's treasures of art, the dawn has come, Aurora has started on her course out of the realm of chaos and darkness.

But the female forms which should harbinger her car and scatter flowers on the way, and bear the torch and crown the victor, these yet delay to appear, and are absent from the picture.

Finally, there is a side of the life of women of the middle and lower classes in Rome, of which I cannot speak, and yet which cannot be passed over in silence without conveying a most false impression of their condition. My information has been derived from too many and too well-experienced residents in Rome to leave much doubt on my mind concerning the awful demoralization which prevails among men and women. In a city with a population of less than 200,000 souls, the existence of nearly 30,000 celibates is an element of hopeless disorder. The priestly government is *prudish*, as if composed of old maids. No flowers may be sold by women; no female ballet-dancers may appear, save in ridiculous drapery; every statue in the galleries is made what they deem decent; and, when I ventured to suggest that the infant schools should admit little girls of three to eight, to learn with little boys of the same age, I was told the Government would close the school at once were such a flagrant impropriety to be attempted. Yet, that the present Pope is himself a man of unimpeachable morals is a subject of almost boastful surprise; and that *many* of his cardinals, or priests and monks, follow his good example, no one seems to believe for a moment. But let us draw a veil over the secrets of this "City of

Destruction," and remember that men cannot set aside God's laws, soul and body, and make religion a cloak for tyranny and wrong, and, after all, leave those who endure such things in a state of moral health and simple piety. Despotism and hypocrisy would not be what they are, could they brood over a nation for ages, and be inhaled by it in every breath like a malaria, and yet leave no fever, no plague behind them, to tell of their poisoned bane. Outraged nature vindicates itself always, and religion, parodied and blasphemed, becomes a curse.

# ESSAY VI.

## WORKHOUSE SKETCHES.

*Reprinted from Macmillan's Magazine, April, 1861.*

It is not as to a scene of touching pathos or tragic interest that we invite our readers, in asking them to examine the condition of our Workhouses. There *is* pathos there, and many an unwritten tragedy. Often have we thought, in hearing the tales so simply told from many a bed of suffering, "Talk of 'The Romance of the Peerage!' 'The Romance of the Workhouse' would offer many a stranger and more harrowing incident." But these interests come later. We crave the reader's attention on this plea only: It is a DUTY laid on us all. In other countries the condition of the destitute poor is mostly determined by Government. *Here* the whole community is answerable for their treatment. No system of democratic rule has ever been devised which, so effectually as the New Poor Law, casts the responsibility of action on the whole population, male and even female. What if it should some day be proved that under few despotisms have worse evils flourished?

In the present paper we cannot pretend to make anything like an exhaustive survey of the subject of the Poor Laws generally. We shall merely attempt a brief inquiry into three of the leading branches of workhouse arrangement, and state in conclusion the plans suggested, or in operation, for the removal of the more important evils in them.

We assume that the Poor Laws have a treble aim. 1st. They should repress pauperism, by making the lives of the vicious and idle disgraceful and wearisome. Thus he who is yet outside the workhouse may be spurred to industry and frugality, by knowing that it is no Castle of Indolence, but a stern mill-round of labour which awaits him if he enter there, and the pauper himself, if redeemable, may be goaded to better habits. 2dly. The Poor Laws should provide for the education of orphan and friendless children in such a manner as should secure them against becoming either criminals or paupers (as their parents commonly have been), and should fit them to earn their bread honestly. 3dly. The Poor Laws should extend to the sick, the aged, the disabled, to all who have no other asylum, and whose present case is helpless and suffering, a shelter which should partake of none of the *penal* elements which belong to the treatment of the idle and vicious pauper.

Such being, it is assumed, the legitimate ends of a Poor Law, it remains to be considered whether on the whole the system commonly adopted effects any of these objects in a reasonably satisfactory degree.

First, then—Is pauperism repressed by our treatment of adult able-bodied paupers, male and female?

A pauper we may define to be "a person who *can* work, but *will not* work without coercion:" one who might have supported himself independently by his labour, but has been degraded by idleness or vice to fling himself on the community for maintenance. To those who properly belong to this class it is obvious that indulgent treatment is no real charity in the highest sense of the word. A workhouse where they may gossip and idle, and drone and grumble, is neither a threat nor a correction. On the other hand, the difficulty which already harasses us in our gaols—to make confinement therein really penal, while forbearing all cruelty and affording all the means of health—is still more serious in the case of workhouses, where there is no crime to be punished, only the negative fault of idleness to be repressed.

On the whole, perhaps, as regards the *male* able-bodied paupers, the treatment pursued is less injudicious, and its results less unsatisfactory than in any other branch of workhouse discipline. Even here, however, the state of stagnation and hopelessness in which life is passed ought surely to be combated by the introduction of some system of rewards which should afford hope to the meritorious, and some penalties of a negative kind which should make the indolent feel that their position here was worse than that of the industrious. Captain Crofton has suggested that his system of marks, which has been found to work so wonderfully well among the convicts of Ireland, should be tried with some modifications in the workhouses. We should wish to see this subject properly considered.

But, whatever may be our judgment of the treatment of the male able-bodied paupers, very decidedly condemnatory must be our conclusion as regards the management of *female* adults, for whom it may be truly said that a residence in the workhouse is commonly moral ruin. The last rags and shreds of modesty which the poor creature may have brought in from the outer world are ruthlessly torn away, ere many weeks are past, by the hideous gossip over the degrading labour of oakum-picking, or in the idle lounging about the "women's yard." It is a common assertion that proper separations are made among the women, and the well-conducted freed from the contamination of the degraded. But, except in a few country unions, this rarely holds good, and perhaps could hardly be expected to do so. The case of one girl at this moment in a London workhouse (a case which we are sure might be paralleled in half the unions in England) offers to us a contemplation quite as horrible as if we were accustomed to shut up our destitute children in a fever hospital or a lazar-house. The girl of whom I speak had been decently educated in a district school. Forced to go into the workhouse, and there conducting herself irregularly, she was threatened with some usual penalty. "I shall take my discharge," she answered, "and go out of the house." "But how will you support yourself, my poor girl?" inquired the kindly-disposed master. The answer was horrible enough—she indicated bluntly the sinful "livelihood," whose secret she had learned since she came to the workhouse.*

Every master and matron could multiply cases like this, and corroborate the assertion that a "girl is ruined if once she passes into the adult ward." In well-ordered houses efforts are always made to save the children by passing them directly from school to service. But what then are the places which we support at public cost, and wherein it is contamination for a girl once to set her foot?

Again, for these miserable fallen women themselves. What are we doing to save *them*, now they have been cast up by the Dead Sea of vice, and left stranded for a time within our reach upon the shore? Here and there a few efforts are made, and warm, kind hands stretched out to draw them up. But usually we leave these most miserable beings unaided in their sin and shame—sin felt now, perhaps for the first time, in all its horror, under that iron monotony

* Workhouse Visiting Journal. No. 11, p. 532.

of life, and bound to the company of souls lost like their own. The chaplain of a large union once described to us a scene which has haunted us ever since—a ward full of these "unfortunates," locked up together through the whole blessed summer time, wrangling, cursing, talking of all unholy things, till, mad with sin and despair, they danced, and shouted their hideous songs in such utter shamelessness and fury that none dared to enter their den of agony.

Now for the second object of the Poor Laws—the education of the young. How do we succeed in our proper aim of cutting off the entail of pauperism, and making the child of the drunken father or profligate mother an honest member of society?

It must be admitted that we have great difficulties to contend with in this undertaking; for the poor children are commonly physically burdened with disease inherited from their parents, or acquired in their own neglected infancy. Perhaps it is true that, in the inscrutable mysteries of Providence, there is also a moral proclivity to the coarser vices in such children, while the apparently happier lot of others is to win the heavenly goal through less miry paths of trial. However this may be, it is certain the pauper child requires very especial care. He needs good food and clothing to strengthen and purify his frame from the probable taint of scrofula; and he needs much tenderness and kindness of treatment, to draw out the affections and sentiments which will have to contend with a low organization.

Are these cares for body and mind really taken? Assuredly they are in some unions; and the healthy happy children are the just pride of the benevolent guardians. But all the experience we have been enabled to obtain, after long attention to the subject, and the visitation by ourselves and friends of a vast number of workhouses, leads us to the sad conclusion that these well-managed unions form the exceptions and not the rule. The pauper children in the majority of workhouses are *not* properly cared for. They are poorly fed, considering their constitutional depression, poorly clad, considering their cold abodes, and not only have no proper encouragement given them to the healthy sports of childhood, but are effectually debarred from them. Well can we recall how this fact struck us for the first time on seeing a group of children in a workhouse in the country, turned for our inspection into their "play-ground." Rarely have we beheld so dismal a sight; for the ugly yard miscalled by that pleasant name was five inches deep in coarse gravel, through which walking was difficult, and running impossible, even had not each poor little creature been weighed down like a galley-slave by a pair of iron-shod shoes as heavy as lead. The poor babes stood huddled in a corner, scared and motionless, when bidden by the matron in an unctuous manner to "play as usual, my dears!" We tried to play ourselves, but were utterly foiled by those sad childish looks. Our companion, the wife of the chairman of that union, promised a carriage load of toys next week. May she have remembered that promise to the poor little ones, to whom life had never yet brought such wonders as a ball or skipping rope! Perhaps it was too late already to teach them what such sports might be.

A number of unions since visited, and many inquiries from experienced persons, have confirmed our impression that, in the usual treatment of children in workhouses, there is terrible disregard of the natural laws of a child's being, and that the consequences are most piteous and fatal. We cannot multiply examples; but the following little sketch given us by a friend, of her impressions of one of the rare gala-days of workhouse children, will sufficiently convey the general results of our investigations:—

"The first time I made acquaintance with the children of C—— Workhouse School, I went with some friends to see them receive presents of toys, sugar-plums, &c., collected for distribution among them by some kind-hearted ladies. We began with the nursery, where the babies and children under three years old are kept. It was a cheerless sight enough, though the room was large and airy, and clean as whitewash could make it, and the babies—there were about twenty altogether—showed no sign of ill-usage or neglect. Most of them looked healthy and well fed, and all scrupulously neat and tidy.

"But it was the unnatural stillness of the little things that affected me painfully. They sat on benches hardly raised from the floor, except a few who were lying on a bed in a corner of the room. All remained perfectly grave and noiseless, even when the basket of toys was brought in and placed in the midst of the circle. There was no jumping up, no shouting, no eager demand for some particularly noisy or gaudy plaything. They held out their tiny hands, and took them when they were bid, just looked at them listlessly for a minute, and then relapsed into dulness again, equally regardless of the ladies' simulated expressions of delight and surprise made for their imitation, or the good clergyman's exhortation to them 'to be good children, and deserve all the pretty things the kind ladies gave them.' I saw only two children who looked really pleased, and understood how to play with the toys given them; and they, I was told, had only been in the house a few days.

"I went to the bed, where three tiny little things were lying fast asleep; a fourth was sitting up wide awake, looking demurely at the strangers and unwonted display of toys, but not asking for anything. She was a pretty little girl of some two years old, with curly flaxen hair, and soft blue eyes,—a fair delicate little creature, who seemed made to be some fond mother's pet, but with the same languid spiritless look all the other children wore. I lifted her from the bed, and tried hard to bring a brighter expression to the childish face. I gave her one of the gayest toys, but it soon dropped from her passive hand. I showed her my watch; she looked and listened as I bade her, but gave no sign of pleasure. 'Ah,' said the nurse, 'that one's an orphan, and never knowed father or mother. She don't understand being made of or petted.' Poor little friendless one, and must she pass through all her desolate childhood, ignorant of what love or petting means? God help her! It was very pitiful to look at that innocent's face, and to think that it might be no look of love would ever rest on it! As I put her down again on the bed, I kissed her, whispering at the same time some words of baby endearment, and then she nestled a little closer to me, and looked up into my eyes with the first faint glimmer of a smile on her lips, as if my words and looks had roused some answering feeling in her baby heart. I do not think any one could have borne that appealing wistful gaze unmoved. I confess my heart felt very heavy, as I left her to relapse again into that mournful gravity, more touching to see in such young creatures than tears or noisy complaints. I must repeat again that I saw no signs of harshness or unkindness on the part of the nurses; but they were both old women, one paralytic; and it is naturally their first object to hush their charges into the state of stupid, joyless, inactivity which gives them the least fatigue and trouble.

'Goodness' and dull quiet are with them synonymous terms. I remembered the many complaints made to us by mistresses of workhouse girls, 'that those girls never so much as knew how to handle an infant, and could not be trusted for a moment alone with the children;' and I longed to turn some of the elder girls from the school into the nursery, for at least some hours every week, under the charge of some good, motherly woman, who would teach them, both by precept and example, how to manage young children. I am told this plan has been tried in some workhouses, and found to succeed. Surely, it would be well to adopt it in all.

"Leaving the nursery, strewed with neglected rattles, rag-dolls, &c., we passed on to the large schoolroom, where all the children—girls, boys, and infants—were to be regaled with tea and plum-cake. The room was, like the other, spotlessly clean and tidy, as were also the children, who stood in long hushed rows before the tables, waiting to sing their grace before they began. The children of the infant school were as still and solemn as the babies—not a smile among them. A little fellow, half hidden by a huge round plum-cake, which stood on the table before him, attracted my attention by his woe-begone face, and piteous efforts to repress an occasional sob. He was one of the healthiest-looking of all the children there, with a brown, rosy face, sturdy brown legs, and fat, dimpled arms—a great contrast to some of his poor, pallid, stunted companions. I lingered behind the rest of the party to ask what ailed him. The sobs came louder, as he faltered out, 'Mammy!' I enlarged on the glories of the coming Christmas-tree, hoping to divert his mind from his grief for a little; but my eloquence was quite wasted; he only looked up and wailed out 'Mammy, mammy!' The sugar-plum I gave him was disdainfully thrown on the floor, as he begged, in passionate, broken accents, to be taken to 'mammy.' I was quite at a loss; but the mistress came up to us, and quieted him with the often repeated and often broken promise, that, if Jemmy would be a good boy, and leave off crying, she would take him very soon to see his mammy. The poor little fellow manfully choked down his sobs, and sat with eager black eyes fixed on the mistress, evidently trying hard to show her how good he was, in hopes of earning the promised reward.

"In answer to my questions, the mistress told me that Jemmy had only been in the house two days. He was brought in with his mother, a respectable woman from the country, who had been forced by adverse circumstances to seek shelter in the workhouse. She further said, it was hard work getting mother and child apart. 'He was her only one, and they had never been separated for so much as a day before, and, though he was three years old, he clung like a baby to her, and she, poor soul, was fretting worse for Jemmy than Jemmy was for her.' No doubt, the boy will soon get used to do without his mother's daily love and care, and be satisfied with the weekly visits which children in the workhouse schools are allowed to pay to their parents; but she will have many a sore struggle before she can learn patiently to resign her only child to strangers' scant care and tenderness. I suppose the separation between mothers and children must exist; but I never felt so forcibly its hardship in particular cases. The perfect indifference with which the matron, a good-natured looking woman, talked of both mother and boy's distress, showed she was too well used to such scenes.

"While I was occupied with Jemmy, the children were standing quiet and silent before the yet untouched tea and plum-cake, listening to a long discourse from one of the clergymen, interspersed with anecdotes of sweet children, who unfortunately all died while still of very tender years, which it might, perhaps, have been better to defer till after the good things were disposed of. However, they were all too well drilled to manifest any signs of impatience, except one very small boy, who, after staring hard at his hot bowl of tea, was suddenly inspired by the idea that it was meant as a bath for his blue, cold hands, and forthwith plunged them in, looking round at his companions with proud satisfaction, in spite of a whisper of 'Naughty boy! See to him, then!' addressed to him by an older and better-informed child.

"At last the speeches were over, and the grace very

nicely sung, and a refreshing clatter of spoons and mugs, and subdued voices, succeeded. . . . . I believe they all enjoyed themselves in their way; but still the difference between their general bearing and that of ordinary National-school children was very striking and very sad. By far the greater number had a depressed, downcast, and spiritless look, almost as if they already felt themselves to belong to an inferior and despised class, and would never have energy even to try to rise above it. Surely it would be well not to go on herding pauper children constantly together, but to let them attend some National-school (as is done at Upton-on-Severn, and a few other unions), and so be mixed, for some hours every day, with *non-pauper* children?"

Let us turn now to a stage beyond early childhood, and judge how the workhouse system acts in education. I must confine myself to the case of the girls, lest the subject should surpass all bounds, and also because the tougher nature of boys enables them to escape with far less injury.

A few days ago a tradesman who had taken from a workhouse school a girl distinguished there for her good qualities, remarked to us with no little indignation, "I don't know why we build reformatories and penitentiaries, and then rear these workhouse girls on purpose to fill them! What *can* happen to them when they are not able to earn a penny by honest labour? This girl has been with me three months, and my wife teaches her all she can, but she is like a fool. We cannot trust her to mind the baby, or sweep the room, or light the fire. She breaks every bit of crockery she touches. If we send her a message she cannot find her way down two streets. Poor people cannot afford to keep such a servant; but, if we part with her, what will become of her?—She is sure to go to ruin."

Now this is precisely what happens to these workhouse girls by hundreds every year in this kingdom. It is a most awful consideration how we leave these helpless creatures to almost inevitable destruction actually by system. We teach them, indeed, to read and write, and sew and sing hymns. All that part of their education is probably quite as good as what is given in the day-schools of the ordinary poor. Also we teach them that portion of religion which may be conveyed in the form of question and answer by rote from a sharp "certified" teacher (generally armed with a cane) and a class of small scholars deeply interested in the employment of that theological instrument. But, if such literary and religious instruction as this be the creditor side of the account, what is the debtor one? It is only the sum of all that makes human nature (more emphatically *woman's* nature) beautiful, useful, or happy! Her moral being is left wholly uncultivated,—the little domestic duties and cares for aged parent or baby brother are unknown. She possesses nothing of her own, not even her clothes or the hair on her head! How is she to go out inspired with respect for the rights of property, and accustomed to control the natural impulses of childish covetousness? Worse than all, the human affections of the girl are all checked, and with them almost inevitably those religious ones, which naturally rise through the earthly parent's love to the Father in heaven. The poor workhouse girl is "the child of an institution"—not of a human mother! Nobody calls her by her Christian name, or treats her in any way as if she individually were of any interest to them. She bears her surname, if she luckily possess one, and the name of some neighbouring lane or field if she be a foundling. She is driven about with the rest of the dreary flock from dormitory to school-room, and from school-room to workhouse-yard—not harshly or unkindly, perhaps, but always as one of a herd, whether well or ill-cared for. She is nobody's "Mary" or "Kate" to be *individually* thought of, talked to, praised, or even perhaps impatiently scolded and punished. What matter? There would have been love at the bottom of the mother's harshness. For the workhouse girl, for "Harding" or "Oakfield," there is no question of love; and youth itself is shorn of every ray of warmth and softness as the poor creature grows up, with her cropped hair and hideous dress, and too often with her face seamed and scarred by fell disease. As to knowing anything really useful, her mind is as blank as the white-washed walls of the dreary yard which her hapless infancy has had for its playground and its whole portion in God's world. The apparent stupidity of these girls when they go out to service, as we have said, is something deplorable—though easily understood when we remember how impossible it is for them to learn by intuition such simple "arts of life" as the lighting of fires, roasting meat, hushing babies, and touching utensils more liable to breakage than tin mugs and workhouse platters. The excellent ladies who have founded St. Joseph's Institute, near Dublin, for the purpose of employing these poor girls in a safe and happy home, have revealed to us the most grotesquely touching anecdotes of the ignorance of their young charges. "One day," says the kind lady, "soon after A. B.'s arrival in the establishment, having been instructed in the art of laying the table, and other branches of the service, she was desired to bring up the potatoes for dinner. Very obediently she accepted the function, and accordingly produced the potatoes—*in the pot!*"—"The greater number of our girls had never been in an ordinary dwelling-house, and their awkwardness on entering one was both provoking and ludicrous. The use of knives and forks was unknown to them; the hall-mat seldom failed to trip them up; they had not presence of mind enough to carry a can of water, and it required practice and experience to enable them to get up and down stairs without falling."—It was soon discovered that a course of rudimental object-lessons should be gone through before one of these girls (averaging in age 16½) could be trusted to execute the most trifling order or commission. What could be expected from a girl who had never seen a railway train, and could not contain her terror and surprise at being put into one? or from another who had indeed seen snow on the roofs and flagways of the union mansion, yet innocently asked, on finding the whole country white after a fall, 'How will the *dust* be got off the trees?'"—"Very difficult it is to teach these girls the value of property; their utter indifference, no matter what amount of mischief they may achieve, is equally perplexing and tantalizing to those in charge of them."*

Among these Irish girls the evils of workhouse treatment seem to have produced more fatal results even than all the stupidity common to their class in England. The Superior of a large convent in Dublin herself assured us that fifty girls whom she had taken from one of the Dublin unions had proved far more vicious and unmanageable than the two hundred *convicts* placed under the charge of her order in a neighbouring establishment. There is a peculiarly ferocious scream, really worthy of wild beasts, practised among these wretched girls whenever a mutiny takes place. It is commonly known in Ireland as the Poorhouse Howl! Few things can be conceived more shocking than the state of affairs revealed by a

* St. Joseph's Industrial Institute, p. 10.

letter from the Poor Law Commissioners to the guardians of the South Dublin Union, 9th January, 1861, wherein permission is granted, in consideration of the outrageous conduct of the young females in the workhouse, to expel them from the house—*i.e.*, to turn them on the streets! Must not these guardians shudder to reflect that many of these girls have been under their charge from early infancy? If they *are* so hideously and hopelessly depraved that there is nothing left for them but the streets, in God's name, we ask, *on whom* lies the blame?

In England the workhouse girls are rather depressed and stupefied than rendered thus defiant, but the result is the same in the end. When they go out to service they disgust their employers. The wretched girl is incapable, idle, insolent, and is treated perhaps harshly, perhaps with that worst cruelty which disregards her moral safety and sends her out at wrong times and places. The experience of agents appointed to help some of these children in one large city has revealed also that they are subjected to the most abominable injustice in the withholding of their pittance of wages. The girl soon learns on her errands through the streets that there is another way of earning her bread than in this drudgery of service—a far easier way they tell her.—A few years later the hapless friendless creature, now a woman ruined and broken down, goes back to the dreary workhouse where her joyless childhood was wasted. This time she is sent, not to the school, but to the "Black Ward!"*

A better day, however, we trust, is dawning for these pauper children. For some time back the London unions have been alive to the necessity of having schools for their children out of town and separate from the workhouses. There are five of these district schools around London, containing in all 7,000 children; and Liverpool, Manchester, and Leeds have followed the example. The house, certified as an industrial school, opened by the Honourable Mrs. Way, at Brockham, near Reigate, where workhouse girls from twelve years old are trained as servants, and Miss Louisa Twining's Home, in New Ormond Street, for girls from fifteen to twenty-five, from London workhouses, promise much higher advantages again than the district schools. *Here* indeed the "entail of pauperism" may, we trust, be fairly cut off, and all the degrading circumstances of the pauper life removed. The girls are brought into smaller communities, where the indispensable element of individual care and feeling is brought to bear on their young hearts; and the nature of the house itself permits the practice of those housewifely duties which cannot be learned in the bare wards and among the machinery of huge troughs and boilers of a workhouse laundry

* "In one metropolitan union, inquiries being made concerning eighty girls who had left the workhouse, and gone to service, it was found that *every one* was on the streets."—*The Workhouse Orphan.*

and kitchen. For moral reasons also the smaller aggregations of girls are altogether preferable. As the late J. C. Symons, Her Majesty's Inspector of Schools, confessed, "Whenever the Legislature establishes district schools it will be well to consider whether the girls' schools ought not to be very limited in size. There is reason to fear that any large groups of girls are liable to become demoralized." In speaking of the present state of things in the large district schools, Miss Twining most justly remarks:—

"It is an *unnatural* system, and one entirely opposed to the order of God's providence as displayed in the arrangements of family life. Not only is it very difficult, if not impossible, to organize an establishment containing 500 or 1,000 persons so as in any way to resemble a family household, even as regards its material arrangements; but it is *absolutely* impossible to introduce into it the elements of family life, which we maintain are essential to the development and well-being of the woman's nature. The necessary scale on which all the operations are conducted (combined with the total absence of all private property), leads to habits of waste and reckless consumption, which are totally incompatible with the future career of the girl, who is destined first for service in a small household, and afterwards will most probably become the poor wife of a labouring man. Establishments of these dimensions must also be served by an army of officials, in whom it is almost in vain to look for the element that will supply the place of home and family affections and sympathies to the poor outcast girl. We are far from saying that there are no remedies to be found for many of the evils which we have alluded to, as at present impeding the full benefit of district pauper schools, and still farther from implying that with all their defects they are not immeasurably superior to the pauperising 'workhouse school;' but we would earnestly ask those who have the power in their hands to pause before they consent to multiply, at an enormous cost, schools containing under one roof and one management 1,000 or 1,600 children,* especially when at the head of this internal management is placed a man and woman who have previously only filled the post of workhouse master and matron.

"The *womanly element* is sorely needed in these institutions; and it is most earnestly to be desired, not only that there should be a council of ladies to confer with the matron on such matters as come within the province of women, but also that there should be *women inspectors* appointed and sanctioned to take cognizance of the education and progress of the girls, both morally and industrially.

"It is one of the most hopeful signs of the present time that so strongly are these convictions beginning to make themselves felt, that 'homes' for poor girls of the workhouse class are beginning to appear here and there through the country. We feel convinced

* Hanwell is built to contain 1,600 children.

that these are based upon a true and sound principle, and that their multiplication is earnestly to be desired. A motherly care and love, combined with thorough training in humble and household duties, and supplemented by a *continued watchful supervision* on leaving the house, surely provides, as far as human wisdom and thoughtful foresight can provide, for the successful start in life and future career of the poor friendless pauper girl; and we believe we are not presumptuous in looking for a large amount of success from the further development of such efforts."

All that is required for the success of this noble experiment is that the guardians should be enabled to pay to well-qualified ladies, or societies, who undertake to found such houses, the same amount which the girls now cost them in the workhouse. By the present order of the Poor Law Board, the guardians can give only the usual amount of *out-door* relief to girls who may be received as inmates of the house, and private charity must supply the remainder of the expense. But it is not just that the matter should remain on this footing, and we trust that the necessary alterations in the Poor Law will be considered at the approaching discussion in Parliament.*

A temporary expedient, which has been tried in one city with entire success, we would earnestly commend to the attention of our readers who have time to bestow on a task wherein a vast amount of *pre-*

* This has actually been done. (1863.)

*ventive* good may be performed with no outlay of money. It is simply this—that in every union ladies should make themselves acquainted (through the workhouse master or otherwise) with the addresses of girls immediately on their being sent out to service. They should then call on each mistress, express their interest in their little servant, and request permission for her to attend a Sunday afternoon class for workhouse girls. *Invariably* it has been found that the mistresses take in good part such visits, made with proper courtesy, and are led to greater consideration for their servants and attention to guard them against moral dangers. *Usually*, also, they have gladly availed themselves of the Sunday-school, which, of course, affords an admirable "basis of operations" for all sorts of good, religious and secular, to these poor children. The main object is effected either way; the girls feel they have a friend whose influence is wholly a moral one, and whose hand is ready to hold them up in the terrible dangers which attend their lot.

Finally, how do we accomplish the third end of the Poor Law, and afford support and comfort *void of all penal element*, towards the sick and helpless who have no other asylum?

Let it be understood that there are many workhouses where this end is effectually accomplished, and many more where the intention to do it is sincere, though the absence of the female element of thoughtfulness for details and tenderness for infirmity *in the very place which the sternest contemners of the sex declare to be woman's proper post, namely, at the bedside of the sick and dying*—the absence, we say, of this element, constantly neutralizes the good intentions of the board. Further, however, than this. The fundamental system of workhouse management is incompatible with proper care of the sick. The infirmary is an *accident* of the house, not its main object; and proper hospital arrangements are consequently almost impracticable. The wards are hardly ever constructed for such a purpose as those of a regular hospital would be, with proper attention to warmth, light, and ventilation. In some cases their position with regard to the other buildings entails all sorts of miseries on the patients —as, for example, the terrible sounds from the wards for the insane. In the courtyard of one metropolitan workhouse, carpet-beating is done as a work for the able-bodied paupers. The windows of the sick and infirm open on this yard, and during the summer cannot be opened because of the dust. In another court, a blacksmith's shed has been erected close under the windows of the infirmary, and the smoke enters when they are opened, while the noise is so violent as to be quite bewildering to a visitor. Can we conceive what it must be to many an aching head in those wretched rooms?

The furniture of the workhouse infirmaries is commonly also unsuited to its destination. The same rough beds (generally made with one thin mattress laid on iron bars) which are allotted to the rude able-bodied paupers, are equally given to the poor, emaciated, bed-ridden patient, whose frame is probably sore all over, and whose aching head must remain, for want of pillows, in a nearly a horizontal position for months together.* Hardly in any workhouse is there a chair on which the sufferers in asthma or dropsy, or those fading away slowly in decline, could relieve themselves by sitting for a few hours, instead of on the edges of their beds, gasping and fainting from weariness. Arrangements for washing the sick, and for cleanliness generally, are most imperfect. We cannot venture to describe the disgusting facts of this kind known to us as existing even in metropolitan workhouses, where neither washing utensils are found, nor the rags permitted to be retained which the wretched patients used for towels. Again, in other workhouses, cleanliness is attempted to an extent causing endless exasperation of disease to the rheumatic sufferers and those with pulmonary affections, to whom the perpetual washing of the floor is simply fatal.† In new country workhouses the walls

* A very simple invention might be used by charitable ladies at trifling expense to relieve this last misery. A knitted bed-rest, the shape of a half-shawl, five feet six inches long, and two feet deep in the middle, affords the most wonderful comfort. It should be made of common knitting-cotton, and tied by double tapes at the end to the ends of the bed, then passed round the patient's back, to which it forms a support like a cradle.

† Ought not the floors of all sick wards to be *waxed*, so as to

of these sick rooms are commonly of stone—not plastered, but constantly whitewashed—and the floor not seldom of stone also. Conceive a winter spent in such a prison: no shutters or curtains, of course, to the windows, or shelter to the beds, where some dozen sufferers lie writhing in rheumatism, and ten or fifteen more coughing away the last chances of life and recovery.

But even the unfitness of the wards and their furniture is second to the question of medical aid and nursing. The salaries usually given to workhouse surgeons are low, the pressure for employment in the medical profession being so great as to induce gentlemen to accept wholly inadequate remuneration. But low as they are, with very rare exceptions, they are made to include the cost of all the drugs ordered to the patients! It would seem as if the mere mention of such a system were enough to condemn it. Underpaid and overworked, it is impossible to expect that the labour and the cost of exhibiting the more expensive medicines can be *ordinarily* undergone. In many cases we believe it would swallow up the whole miserable salary of the surgeon and go far beyond it, were he to give to the pauper sufferers the anodynes they so piteously require, and to the weak, half-starved, scrofulous, and consumptive patients the tonics, cod-

obviate the necessity of washing? The damp is agony to the rheumatic patients, and death to those with consumption or erysipelas.

liver oil, &c., on which their chances of life must depend. Again, there may be the most difficult and intricate cases, requiring all possible skill. In every other hospital the most experienced physicians would attend such cases. Here a young man (necessarily at the outset of his profession, or he would not accept such a position) has to decide everything for himself. What would the board think of being continually called on to pay consultation fees to the leading surgeons and physicians in the neighbourhood?

It is the received theory that it is in the power of the medical officer of each union to order *all* that his patients require; and guardians perpetually boast that they never refuse to countersign such orders. The nature of the case, however, is pretty obvious. The surgeon knows what things will, and what will *not* be sanctioned, and rarely attempts the useless task of collision with the board, in which it almost invariably happens that along with many benevolent guardians are others whose sole object is to "keep down the rates" at any cost of human suffering.

Besides the anomalous arrangements of wards and medical attendance in workhouses, which are actually hospitals without proper hospital supervision, there remains a third source of misery to the inmates—the *nurses.* It is easy to understand that the difficulty of obtaining good nurses in ordinary hospitals is doubled here. Indeed it is rarely grappled with at all; for women hired by the board are so invariably brought into collision with the master and matron, that even the kindest of such officials say (and probably say truly) that it is best to be content with the pauper nurses, over whom at least they can exercise some control. The result is that, in an immensely large proportion of houses, the sick are attended by male or female paupers who are placed in such office without having had the smallest preparatory instruction or experience, and who often have the reverse of kindly feelings towards their helpless patients. As *payments* they usually receive allowances of beer or gin, which aid their too common propensity to intoxication.

A good deal of misapprehension, we believe, exists as to the class of persons who are inmates of the sick wards of our workhouses. They are very frequently quite of another and higher order than that of the able-bodied paupers—their disease, not any vice or idleness, having brought them to their present condition. Especially among the women do we find the most piteous cases of reduced respectability—widows of tradesmen, upper servants, and even teachers and governesses, joined in one common lot of sordid poverty, and sleeping side by side with poor creatures whose lives have been passed in a hopeless drudgery of labour—in selling apples in the streets, or in lower avocations still. All the heaviest misery, in fact, of our country *drains* into the workhouse as to the lowest deep; and only by meeting it there can we hope to relieve the worst of our social tragedies.

A few notes from the memoranda of Miss Elliot will enable the reader who has never visited a workhouse infirmary to form some judgment of its inmates.

"I went first to — workhouse to visit an old woman whom I had known for some time before she entered it. She had been more of a companion than maid to an invalid lady, and had the manners of a well-bred and well-informed person. Her husband was unfortunate in business, and left her with a daughter, who herself married and died, leaving the grandmother to support her son. I am not writing their history, or I might tell of patience and faith from which we all might learn. At last the old woman, almost blind and crippled with rheumatism, could no longer do anything for herself—the boy entered the navy, and she took shelter in the workhouse. Her shame at receiving me there was at first very painful both to herself and to me; but she is thankful now, and talks of her comforts and of God's goodness in providing her with shelter and food. Her heart was cheered after two years by her grandson's return and offer to try and support her out of the house; but she has few days, she hopes, to stay there now, and she will not burden his young life. . . . In the next bed lies an old woman of nearly eighty, paralysed, and, as I thought, gone beyond the power of understanding me. Once, however, when I was saying 'good bye' before an absence of some months, I was attracted by her feeble efforts to catch my attention. She took my hand and gasped out, 'God bless you; you wont find me when you come back. Thank you for coming.' I said most truly that I had never been any good to her, and how sorry I was I had never spoken to her, 'Oh, but I see your face; it is always a great pleasure and seems bright. I was praying for you last night. I don't sleep much of a night. I thank you for coming.' . . A woman between fifty and sixty dying of liver disease. She had been early left a widow, had struggled bravely, and reared her son so well that he became foreman at one of the first printing establishments in the city. His master gave us an excellent character of him. The poor mother unhappily got some illness which long confined her in another hospital; and when she left it her son was dead—dead without her care and love in his last hours. The worn-out and broken-down mother, too weak and hopeless to work any longer, came to her last place of refuge in the sick ward of the workhouse. There day by day we found her sitting on the side of the bed, reading and trying to talk cheerfully, but always breaking down utterly when she came to speak of her son. Opposite to her an old woman of ninety lies, too weak to sit up. One day, not thinking her asleep, I went to her bedside. I shall never forget the start of joy, the eager hand, 'Oh, Mary, Mary, you are come! Is it you at last!' 'Ah, poor dear,' said the women round her, 'she most always dreams of Mary. 'Tis her daughter, ladies, in London; she has written to her often, but don't get any answer.' The poor old woman made many and profuse apologies for her mistake, and laid her head wearily on the pillow where she had rested and dreamed literally for years of Mary.

"Further on is a girl of eighteen, paralyzed, hopelessly, for life. She had been maid-of all work in a family of twelve, and under her fearful drudgery had broken down thus early. 'Oh, ma'am,' she said with bursts of agony, 'I would work; I was always willing to work, if God would let me; but I shall never get well—never!' Alas, she may live as long as the poor cripple who died here last summer, after lying forty-six years in the same bed gazing on the same blank, white wall. The most cheerful woman in the ward is one who can never rise from her bed; but she is a good needlewoman, and is constantly employed in making *shrouds*. It would seem as if the dismal work gave her an interest in something outside the ward, and she is quite eager when the demand for her manufacture is especially great!

"Let us go to the room above, the Surgical Ward, as it is called. Here are some eight or ten patients, all in painful diseases. One is a young girl dying of consumption, complicated with the most awful wounds on her poor limbs. 'But they don't hurt so bad,' she says, 'as any one would think who looked at them, and it will soon be all over. I was just thinking it was four years to-day since I was brought into the

Penitentiary (it was after an attempt to drown herself after a sad life of sin at Aldershott); and now I have been here three years. God has been very good to me, and brought me safe when I didn't deserve it.' Over her head stands a print of the Lost Sheep, and she likes to have that parable read to her. Very soon that sweet, fair young face, as innocent as I have ever seen in the world, will bear no more its marks of pain. Life's whole great tragedy will have been ended, and she is only just nineteen!—A little way off lies a woman dying in severest agonies, which have lasted long, and may yet last for weeks. Such part of her poor face as may be seen expresses almost angelic patience and submission, and the little she can say is all of gratitude to God and man. 'I shall not live to see So-and-so again, but don't let them think I did not feel their kindness. The doctor, too, he is so good to me; he gives me everything he can.' On the box beside her bed there stands usually a cup with a few flowers, or even leaves or weeds—something to which, in the midst of that sickening disease, she can look for beauty. When we bring her flowers her pleasure is almost too affecting to witness. She says she remembers when she used to climb the hedge rows to gather them in the 'beautiful country.'—Opposite this poor sufferer, in the midst of all those aged and dying women, lies a strange little figure asleep on his bed. It is a boy of ten years old, so crippled that his little limbs as he sleeps are all contorted. Nothing could be done for him; so he is left here to live perhaps a few years, and then, no doubt, he must die. He is an orphan, poor child! but many of the women take an interest in him, and he seems so quiet and gentle one can hardly wish him to go among the other children. We bring him little toys now and then. His laugh is very strange—so feeble, and sharp, and short, one wonders almost whether it be a laugh at all —a child's laugh in that chamber of suffering and death!"

The condition of one class of the sick in the workhouse calls, however, for more than pity—for simple justice. They are excluded from the benefits of the free hospitals, not, like the others, by *accident*, but by *rule*. Their sufferings are greatest of any, and no assumption of blame of any kind lies against them. I allude to the Destitute Incurables, for whom only of late a plea for some share of public charity has begun to be urged. We have long gone on quietly admitting that, when cancer, dropsy, or consumption becomes hopeless, the sufferer must be rejected by the hospital in which, while curable, he might have found every comfort. But why have we never dreamed of asking, *Where does he go*, when thus excluded? Where and how are spent the last long months, or perhaps years, of inevitable agony, whose heavy weight it has pleased an inscrutable Providence to lay upon him? Perhaps it has seemed there were too few of such patients to need any special provision. The Registrar-General's report, however, gives us a different idea of the case. Taking the above-named three types of incurable disease alone, we find that upwards of 80,000 persons die of them in England every year. There are other forms of malady—as, for instance, confirmed rheumatism—entailing equally intense and more prolonged suffering. But we will confine ourselves to the 80,000 who die of dropsy, consumption, and cancer, and ask the reader to estimate how many of those under such a visitation must be flung helpless on either their friends or the community for support; and how many of them can be supposed to *have* friends able and willing to nurse and support them through the last months of disease? The answers may vary; but we may safely maintain that at the very lowest computation 30,000 must be driven to die in the workhouses under all the aggravations of their misery which we have described.

It is manifestly hopeless to think of opening hospitals for incurables adequate to such a demand, since, at the lowest rate of 30*l.* per annum, we should need a revenue of 900,000*l.* to support 30,000 patients. A much simpler plan, originated by Miss Elliot, the daughter of the Dean of Bristol, has been urged in Papers read before the Social Science Association, in Glasgow and Dublin.* It is, that the incurables

* Destitute Incurables. By Miss Elliot and Miss Cobbe. (Nisbet and Co.) Price 2*d.*

The Sick in Workhouses. By Frances Power Cobbe. (Emily Faithfull.) Price 2*d.*

in workhouses should henceforth be avowedly distinguished from other paupers; that separate wards should be allotted to them, and that into these wards private charity may be admitted, to introduce whatever comforts may alleviate the sufferings of the inmates. It is conceded that to charge the poor-rates with all the extra expenses which would assimilate the condition of a workhouse infirmary to that of a regular hospital, might involve injustice to the ratepayers. On the other hand, it is maintained that it is still more unjust to incurable patients to exclude them from our 270 splendid free hospitals, and then, when we have driven them into the workhouses, shut them up therein from receiving whatever small alleviations human charity might bring to their inevitable sufferings. Neither is the admission of this principle of voluntary aid into the workhouse system to be looked on in any way as an evil, or disturbance of desirable order. As one of the framers of the Poor Laws has remarked, those laws were designed to form a mere bony skeleton, indicating the form and affording a basis for the *flesh* of voluntaryism to make a living body of national charity. By a fatal result of jealousy and routine, the voluntary element has been too often excluded, and we have only a fearful spectre, haunting with death-like image all the lower vaults of our social fabric. Let free charity be not only permitted, but invited to enter these English Towers of Oblivion (dread as that which frowned over old Byzantium), and a new order of things will swiftly arise for the child and the young woman, for the fallen, the aged, and the sick. Everywhere we *want* the aid of wise men's minds and loving women's hearts; and that they should begin to work among the incurably diseased and dying is *not* the admission of an irregularity to be deplored, but the commencement of a new order joyfully to be inaugurated. Especially we want the presence of women in nearly every department of the workhouse. The guardians, however well disposed, cannot understand either the details of the physical or moral training of the children and young girls, or the proper care of the sick. Everything lies with the matron, and (as one of the most experienced female philanthropists of our age herself assured the writer), "there never yet lived a man whom the matron of an institution could not perfectly deceive respecting every department of her work." The care of infants, the training of young girls, the subduing of harshness by gentleness, the reclaiming of fallen women, the tender care of the suffering and dying—these are the "Rights of Women," given her by God Himself—and woe be to man when he denies them! Monstrous are the evils which inevitably ensue. If for many reasons we cannot wish to see women claim the rights (which they probably possess by common law) to be elected as guardians of the poor, at least let their aid in the workhouse be universally sanctioned and welcomed. We are happy to think that the time is approaching when this principle will be everywhere admitted. Already the Workhouse Visiting Society, founded and maintained mainly by the exertions of Miss Louisa Twining, have obtained entrance into, and are carrying on their visits in, nearly 100 out of the 660 workhouses in England.

To return to the plan for the relief of incurables. It is suggested that in each union, on the wards being set apart for such patients, lady-visitors should collect and apply contributions for the following purposes :—

1st. Furniture. Good spring-beds or air-beds in extreme cases for bedridden patients. Easy-chairs for those who cannot lie down in asthma or dropsy, or, if in decline, are too weak to sit on the usual benches of the ward and so spend all their days in bed. Air cushions and wicker bed cradles for those who have sores, &c. Should the local contributions be insufficient to purchase these articles, applications for grants in aid may be made to Miss Louisa Twining, 13, Bedford Place, Russell Square, London. A central fund for the purpose already exists, opened at Messrs. Twining's, Strand.

2nd. Small refreshments and amusements to be supplied from time to time by the visitors—such as *good* tea (not the usual nauseous mixture called by that name in workhouses), lemonade, fruit, lozenges for those who cough all night to their own misery and that of their neighbours, snuff, a few coloured prints for the walls, and flowers for the window, spectacles for those who need them, and for want of them often remain blind and idle for years together; books, both serious and amusing, to beguile the weary hours. Above all, a little breath of cheer from the outer world —the sight of kindly faces, which, the poor sick souls constantly remark, "look so beautiful and fresh"— and the trifling marks of interest which a kindly visitor spontaneously displays.

3rd. It is hoped that it may be possible to reach the monster evil of unqualified nurses, and to pay from voluntary contributions the salaries of good ones who should be subordinated so completely to the matron as to obviate the existing prejudices and difficulties. Finally, as it is at all times exceedingly difficult to obtain the services of well-qualified nurses, it is hoped that it may prove practicable to train the workhouse girls in the "Homes" for such service, by attaching to the establishments wards for incurable patients who are in need of careful attendance, though able to defray the cost of their own support. Such a class is not rarely to be met, and would be as much benefited as the girls, who (on showing fitness for the task) would receive instruction qualifying them to earn a comfortable livelihood, and to be of essential service to the community.

A circular, embodying the plan of separate wards,

and voluntary aid for incurables, and proffering the services of the Workhouse Visiting Society in carrying it into execution, was lately despatched to every board of guardians in England, and published in the *Times* and many other papers. We are happy to say that it has met with favourable consideration from a great number of unions, and that many have already adopted it and put it in execution.

In concluding this brief and imperfect sketch of the present condition of our workhouses, we have only to repeat the appeal with which we first claimed our reader's attention to the subject. It is a DUTY laid on us all to investigate the action of regulations which we have an immediate (or mediate) influence in making, and which most essentially concern the happiness, the life, and the moral welfare of our fellow-creatures. We *are*, each of us, "our brother's keeper;" never more emphatically so than when we shut him up in the walls of our workhouse! The assertions made in this paper may or may not be just, or founded on sufficient data; but every one who has read them must henceforth know that such abuses *may* be passing in his own immediate neighbourhood, supported by his own elected representative, and maintained by his own money. On him it lies to ascertain whether we have spoken truth or whether what we have said applies to his own union. Let him not think to leave on another man's conscience the weight which must rest at last upon his own—a fearful weight, if it should prove that through his act (*or his negligence of action*) the agonies of the dying have been left unrelieved, the lives of the weak and sick have failed to be saved, and the young souls left helpless in our charge have been suffered to drop into that lowest deep of woman's shame, whose end is the "Black Ward of the Workhouse."

# ESSAY VII.

## THE EDUCATION OF WOMEN, AND HOW IT WOULD BE AFFECTED BY UNIVERSITY EXAMINATIONS.

*A Paper read by the Author, before the Social Science Association, London*, 1862.

THE subject of the Education of Women of the higher classes is one which has undergone singular fluctuations in public opinion. There have been times when England and Italy boasted of the literary attainments of a Lady Jane Grey and a Vittoria Colonna, and there have been times when the Chinese proverb seemed in force, and it was assumed that "the glory of a man is knowledge, but the glory of a woman is to renounce knowledge." For the last half-century, however, the tide seems to have set pretty steadily in the direction of feminine erudition. Our grandmothers understood spelling and writing, Blair's Sermons and long whist. Our mothers to these attainments added French and the pianoforte, and those items (always unimportant in a woman's education), history and geography. In our own youth we acquired, in a certain shadowy way peculiar to the boarding-schools of that remote period, three or four languages and three or four instruments, the use of the globes and of the dumb-bells, moral philosophy and Poonah-painting. How profound and accurate was this marvellous education (usually completed at the mature age of sixteen) it is needless to remark. A new generation has appeared, and he who will peruse the splendid curriculum of one of the Ladies' Colleges, of Bedford Square, or Harley Street, for instance, will perceive that becoming an accomplished young lady is a much more serious affair now than it was in "the merry times when we were young."

The question has now arisen, This wider and deeper education, how far is it to go? Have we reached its reasonable limit, or shall we see it carried much farther? If it be found desirable to push it into higher branches of study and greater perfection of acquirements, how will this best be accomplished? In particular, the grave query has lately been mooted, "Will those University examinations and academical honours, which have long been reckoned all-powerful in advancing the education of men, be found equally efficacious in aiding that of women? Ought they to be opened to female competition, and a Free

Trade in knowledge established between the sexes? Or, on the contrary, does there appear just cause why this door, at all events, should for ever be closed to the possible progress of women?

Before offering a few suggestions on this subject, I crave permission to make some general observations on the present condition of young women of the higher classes, and their special wants at this moment. A knowledge of these wants has alone induced me to obey the request to give such little aid as may be in my power to their efforts after a better state of things. Few indeed can be unaware that they are passing through a transition period of no small difficulty, and that there is urgent need for revision of many of the old social regulations regarding them. No class has felt more than they the rise in the atmosphere of modern thoughts; and where their mothers lived healthily enough in closed chambers, they are stifling. New windows must be opened to the light, new air of heaven admitted, and then we shall see bloom in women's cheeks, and light in their eyes, such as they have never worn before.

The miseries of the poor are doubtless greatest of all, but there are other miseries beside theirs which it behoves us also to consider. The wretchedness of an empty brain is perhaps as hard to bear as that of an empty purse, and a heart without hope as cheerless as a fireless grate. As society is now constituted, no inconsiderable portion of women's lives are aimless and profitless. There are Eugénie Grandets by hundreds in all our towns, and Marianas in Moated Granges in the country, whose existence is no better than that of "the weed on Lethe's banks," and yet who were given by Providence powers whereby they might have become sources of happiness to all around them. For (let us hope it will some time or other be recognised) there *are* purposes in the order of Providence for the lives of single women and childless wives, and they too are meant to have their share of human happiness. Most people prefer to ignore their existence as a class to be contemplated in the education of women, but it is as vain to do so as it is cruel. All of us know enough of those hapless households where the wife, having no children and few home duties, undergoes the most deplorable depreciation of character for want of employment of heart and mind; and her nature, if originally weak and small, shrivels up in petty vanities and contentions; and if strong and high, falls too often blasted by the thunderstorms of passion accumulated in the moveless and unwholesome atmosphere. All of us know those other households, none less hapless, where grown-up daughters, unneeded by their parents, are kept from all usefulness or freedom of action, frittering away the prime of their days in the busy idleness of trivial accomplishments; till, when all energy to begin a new course is gone, the parents die at last, and each one sinks into the typical "Old Maid," dividing her life henceforth in her small lodgings, between "*la medisance, le jeu, et la dévotion.*"

All this is pitiful enough. We may laugh at it; but it is not the less a miserable destiny, and one, moreover, which it is often almost impossible for a young woman to shake off. If she be a Roman Catholic, she may leave her home and go into a nunnery in all honour and credit; but the exchange is perhaps no great gain. If she be a Protestant, friends, parents, neighbours, and all her little world cry out lustily if she think of leaving her father's roof for any end, however good or noble, save only that one sacred vocation of matrimony, for which she may lawfully leave a blind father and dying mother, and go to India with Ensign Anybody. These curiosities of public opinion need surely to be set right. Let me plead with those men and women whose lives are rich and full, whose every hour has its duty or its pleasure, who can say,

> "How beautiful it is to be alive!
> To wake each morn as if the Maker's grace
> Did us afresh from nothingness derive,"

to think of these poor, narrow, withered existences, and not say, "How can we keep women just what we would like—images set up in a niche?" but, "What can we do to give to a vast number of our fellow-creatures all the joys of a useful and honourable life?" Again, there are numbers of young women who are free, so far as the wishes of their parents go, to devote themselves to practical usefulness. But the employment of women of the upper classes is one of the most difficult of achievements. At nearly every door they knock in vain; and, what is worse, they are sometimes told they are unfit for work (even for philanthropic work), *because* they are not soundly educated, or possessed of steady business habits. Yet when they seek to obtain such education, here again they meet the bolted door!

It is needless to go on farther. Enough has been said, I trust, to show that young women (both those possessed of the means of independent maintenance, and those desiring to support themselves by intelligent labour) are sadly in need of some further improvements in their condition. Among the ways in which it may be possible to effect such improvements, a high education manifestly stands foremost—a great good in itself, and needful for nearly all further steps of advance. On this subject also I must say a few words, and notably, to refute some popular misconceptions regarding it.

The idea that there is a natural incompatibility between classical studies and feminine duties, and that a highly-educated lady is necessarily a bad wife and mother, is indeed an idea venerable from its antiquity and wide diffusion. "I would rather make women good wives than teach them Latin," is a favourite species of apothegm, whose parallel, however (for all the sense it possesses), might be found in saying, "I would rather make women good wives than make them eat their breakfasts!" Storing the mind with declensions, or the mouth with tea and toast, are neither of them, in the nature of things, antithetic to becoming a careful housewife and an affectionate companion. As Sydney Smith remarked, "A woman's love for her offspring hardly depends on her ignorance of Greek, nor need we apprehend that she will forsake an infant for a quadratic equation." *A priori*, the thing is not probable, and actually we see that a very different doctrine holds good. Few of us, I think, would fail to cite in their own circles the best cultivated women as precisely those whose homes are the happiest, who exercise therein that spirit of order and love of beauty, and, above all, that sense of the sacredness of even the smallest duties, which comes of true culture of mind. These private examples of moral excellence in studious women we cannot often quote on such occasions as the present. I may be permitted, however, to name two of them who have become household words among us all, and both of whom it has been my rare fortune to know very intimately. They are examples respectively of the two great lines in which a woman's virtue may be best displayed: the home duties of the wife and mother, and the out-of-door duties of the philanthropist.

The woman whose home was the happiest I ever saw, whose aged husband (as I have many times heard him) "rose up and called her blessed" above all, and whose children are among the most devoted, was the same woman who in her youth outstripped nearly all the men of her time in the paths of science, and who in her beloved and honoured age is still studying reverently the wonders of God's Creation,—that woman is Mary Somerville.

And the woman whose philanthropy has been the most perfect, who has done more than any beside to save the criminal and vagrant children of our land, and whose whole time and heart are given to their instruction, that woman is the same who taught Homer and Virgil as assistant in her father's school at eighteen,—that woman is Mary Carpenter.

We now proceed a step farther in our argument. After the examples cited, it may perhaps be assumed as proved that a high education does not in itself unfit women from performing either domestic or philanthropic duties; but that, on the contrary, it is a thing to be desired on every account. Our next position obviously is this: If a high education is to be desired for women, ought it not to be sought for them in those same University studies and honours which have so long proved efficacious in the case of men? Here another objection straightway rises up against us: "A *high* education (it is said) may be desirable for women, but not a *University* education; for that would be to assimilate the training of the two sexes, and any step in such a direction must be fatal, as tending to obliterate the natural differences between them."

A most weighty objection indeed would this be, were it founded on fact.

No *man* can possibly less desire any obliteration of the mental characteristics of the two sexes, than does every woman who has an intelligent care for the welfare of her own. But is such erasure indeed *possible?* Is it not clear enough that the Creator has endowed men and women with different constitutions of mind as of body? and need we be under the slightest apprehension that any kind of education whatever will efface those differences? Education is, after all, only what its etymology implies—the educing, the drawing out, of the powers of the individual. If we, then, draw out a *woman's* powers to the very uttermost, we shall only educe her *womanliness.* We cannot give her a man's powers any more than we can give a man a woman's brilliancy of intuition, or any other gift. We can only educe her God-given *woman's* nature, and so make her a more perfect woman. These differences will, I affirm, come out in every line of woman's expanding powers—in study, quite as much as in all beside. If a woman apply herself to Art, it will be a fresh type of beauty she will reveal. If she devote herself to philanthropic labours, she will not work like a man, from *without*—by outward legislation, but as a woman, from *within*—by the influence of one heart on another. Not by force of will, not by despotic volition does a woman ever do any good. She has abandoned somewhat of her womanhood when she exerts such powers. Even in teaching a class of little children, she rules not by authority, but by winning each little heart to voluntary submission. And in every other work it is the same. Her true victory must ever be an inward one,—a greater and more perfect victory, therefore, than was ever gained by conqueror's sword. And in matters of study it will be the same. Woman learns differently from man; and when she is able to teach, she teaches differently and with different lessons. If ever the day arrives when women shall be able to deal worthily with the subjects of our highest interests, we shall all be the better, I believe, for completing man's ideal of religion and morals by that of woman, and learning to add to his Law of Justice her Law of Love, and to his faith in God's fatherly care, her faith in His motherly tenderness,—that blessed lesson forgotten too long: that "as a woman hath compassion on the son of her womb, even so the Lord hath pity on us all"!

The differences between men and women are co-extensive with their whole natures. A man and a woman are *parallel* to each other, but never *similar*. He is the Right Hand of humanity, and she is the Left. They are *equivalents* to each other, but never *equals*. He is the pound in gold, and she is the twenty shillings in silver. All these differences are innate, unchangeable, ineradicable. It is a perfect caricature of them to represent that some kinds of knowledge are fit for men, and other kinds for women. As well might we say that some kinds of food were fit for one and not the other. It is not *in the truths to be acquired*, but in the *assimilation* of those truths in the mind which receives them, that the difference consists. It is as absurd to try to keep a woman feminine in mind by making her learn French because a man learns Latin, as it would be to try to keep her so in person by making her eat mutton because a man eats beef! Endless are the absurdities of this kind extant among us. Men ought to be well-informed: let women, then, know nothing but trivial accomplishments. Men ought to be strong and healthy: let a woman's cheek (as Burke expresses it) display the charming *morbidezza* of partial disease. A man ought to be brave: let a woman be instructed to dread all things in heaven and earth, from thunder-storms to spiders. Thus it is fondly imagined we are helping Providence to keep women women, and securing the universe against the disorder of their turning into men. Not, however, by narrowing and clipping every faculty—not by pinching her in mental stays, shall we make a true woman. Such processes produce Dolls, not Women; figures very suitable to be set up in haberdashers' shops, to show off bonnets and crinolines, but not such forms as sculptors copy as types of womanly beauty. Our affair is to give nature its fullest, healthiest play and richest culture, and then the result will be what the Lord of Nature has designed—a true Woman; a being, not artificially different from a man, but radically and essentially, because *naturally*, different—his *complement* in the great sum of human nature, not a mere *deduction* from his own share of that sum.

If these views be true, it follows that the highest education we can give will never efface, in the slightest degree, the natural characteristics of a woman's mind. Another argument, however, is here urged against us. It is said, "Let it be granted that you will not make women *masculine* by teaching them Greek and Euclid; yet, it may still appear that Greek and Euclid are very inappropriate studies for women—useless in themselves, if not detrimental in the way supposed. A woman's mind has natural *affinities* to the lighter studies, and *repulsions* to the heavier ones. Let us have an entirely different course of studies, suited to the feminine soul, and then, perhaps, the form of a University education may be beneficial."

Now, that anyone will aver that the subjects of study in any one University are actually the very best possible subjects for women, or even for men, I do not suppose we shall find. But the point is, Who is to decide what is fit for a woman's brain save the owner of the brain herself? Who has a right to decree that the curriculum for the *goose* ought not to be the same as that which collegiate wisdom has appointed for the *gander?* If we were told that soldiers, artisans, or any other class of the community had sought instruction in arithmetic, or any such study, we should hardly think it our business to lay down the law for them: "This is fit for you to learn, and this is unfit; your Bœotian brains may have *affinities* for the multiplication table, but they have certainly *repulsions* for the rule of three." The proof of this particular description of pudding lies exclusively in the eating!

It may be found, indeed, hereafter, that opening up other studies for examination than those at present used, and leaving the option among them free, may be a desirable change, specially beneficial to women. This is quite possible; but in any case the highest masculine studies ought to be left free to a woman, *if* she feel the power and perseverance to undertake them. As Herbert Spencer remarks, "That a woman has *less* powers than a man, is a poor argument why she should be forbidden to use such powers as she *has*." It is a grave mistake to assume that what we judge is the proper pursuit for women in general is the proper one for each in particular, and that we have any just authority to crush individuality displayed in the choice of unusually arduous studies.

The three great revelations of the Infinite One—the True, the Beautiful, and the Good—are all alike in sanctity in themselves. To devote life to the pursuit of any one of them is a noble thing. With respect to the Good we all feel this, and admit that to promote the virtue and happiness of our neighbours is a holy destiny for man or woman. And again, with respect to the Beautiful, we in a degree admit the same for women; and if they display the gifts of Jenny Lind, or Mrs. Browning, or Rosa Bonheur, or Harriet Hosmer, we permit them to study music, or poetry, or painting, or sculpture. But with respect to the True, the rare and noble love of it, the readiness to devote life to its acquirements in abstract and abstruse studies—this is a thing we can hardly bring ourselves to sanction in a woman. Most women care only for the concrete and the personal, and the widest generalizations of philosophy too often interest them only as they concern the small affairs of their families and neighbours. Therefore, *because* few women rise to the love of abstract truth, *no* women are to be permitted to do so? This is utterly absurd. Instead of striving to bring all to the same dead level, we should welcome heartily all earnest devotion to Truth, Beauty, or Goodness, and rejoice in every diversity of gift whereby women may bring their special characteristics into play, and so enrich us all.

If I may hope that by these observations I have removed, in a measure, the objections to women pursuing the solid studies of a University education, I may now proceed to the positive side of the argument, which seems to have received far too little attention from men; namely, that the natural constitution of the female mind renders a solid education peculiarly desirable, and even necessary, to bring out all womanly powers and gifts in proper balance and usefulness. I verily believe that a *man* can infinitely better dispense with sound mental training than a woman. Among the essential differences between the mental constitutions of the two sexes, one of the most obvious is the preponderance in the latter of the intuitive over the reasoning faculties. As it has been facetiously expressed, "When a man has laboriously climbed up step by step to the summit of his argument, he will generally find a woman standing before him on the top. But of how she got there, neither he nor she can give the smallest explanation." This rapid intuition of women may or may not prove a defect. Properly trained and balanced by that carefulness of truth which comes of conscientious study, it is no defect at all, but a great advantage; but unregulated quickness is a peril and misfortune. Jumping at conclusions is a favourite species of feminine steeplechase, with whose sad results we are probably all too familiar. I recollect an instance of it, in which that imperviousness to reason, which affords apparently so much pleasure to spectators when manifested by young ladies, must have been rather trying to the person principally concerned. It happened that an elderly lady, a "true woman" on weak-minded principles, discovered that the gentleman in whose house she resided had kindly paid the insurance for her personal property along with his own at his fire-office. Rousing herself in great indignation, she exclaimed, "He insure my property? He insure *getting my property after my death?* No such thing! I meant to leave him a good legacy, now I will do nothing of the kind—I will alter my will and leave him nothing at all!" Vainly did the unfortunate gentleman endeavour to explain that fire insurances did not insure inheritance of property. Vainly did his friend, a Queen's Counsel of eminence, who had convinced a hundred juries, argue for hours with that irate old lady. Her will was altered, and the legacy revoked! I should like to know the sincere opinion of that gentleman on the desirability of giving a better cultivation to the reasoning faculties of women.

Again, women need solid mental training, not only to amend their reasoning and open their minds to argument, but also to correct the terribly inaccurate and superficial knowledge they now usually think sufficient. If the ladies of the present day proceed in geography too far to ask the celebrated query of one of their grandmothers, "Was Hyder Ali an island or a continent?" and if in physical science they no longer (like another old lady) confine their knowledge of flowers to the Aurora Borealis and the delirium tremens, yet abundance of them are to be found whose ideas of Hyder Ali are of the most hazy description, and whose physical science might be expressed in the exhaustive analysis of another lady: "Plants are divided by botanists into monandria, bulbous roots, and weeds." Modern languages are excellent studies, especially for us women, to whom enforced silence, whether in England or on the Continent, is not supposed to be particularly tasteful. Often have I rejoiced for myself and my fellows, in finding ourselves all over Europe and the East, not only chattering away gaily on our own account, but able to assist our countrymen out of the multitudinous dilemmas to which their ignorance consigned them. Indeed, if any one particular branch of education be liable to the charge of giving to ladies an inconvenient degree of independence of, and even power over the lordly sex, it is precisely this one of modern languages, which on all hands is given as our *specialité*. A certain old saw concerning the "Grey Mare," and her superiority to her masculine companion in harness, is never so forcibly brought to recollection as when we behold the intelligent mother of a family at a railway station or hotel door in Italy or Germany, making all needful payments and arrangements with the utmost fluency and *savoir faire;* while at the rear of her brood of pretty chickens comes Paterfamilias, able to do nothing except carry the umbrellas and "Bradshaws" of the party.

But these same delightful modern languages, does their acquirement afford any mental training similarly beneficial to that which a boy's mind undergoes over his Latin grammar? Speaking from my own sad experience, I must avow it does nothing of the kind, and that it is possible to talk three or four of them while remaining in pristine innocence regarding the cases and tenses of any one.

Lastly, the one noble science which would be the very best corrective of the slovenliness of female instruction, the science of geometry, is nearly utterly neglected. I verily believe that to gain only the idea of what constitutes a mathematical demonstration, and how mathematical reasoning proceeds, would be to many of our minds a clearing up of fog and haze which would brighten the rest of our days.

Now to bring woman's education out of the stage of imperfection in which it stops, it seems evident that some test and standard of perfection is needful. And this test to be sought and applied must be made a goal to which women will strive as ensuring some sort of prize. Scholarships and similar rewards are already used with much benefit at Bedford and other Ladies' Colleges. But the prize which naturally belongs to perfection of attainment is simply its *recognition*,—such public and secure recognition of it as shall make it available for all subsequent purposes. Herein will women find (as men have long found) the sufficient stimulus to strain up to that point, without which, in fact, education must ever be most incomplete. What the education of Oxford and Cambridge would be were there no such things as "Little-go" and "Great-go," no examinations or strivings for degrees, women's education has hitherto been—nay, it has been worse, for it has been stopped at an age earlier than the collegiate education of men begins, and all the best years of study have been lost to her. We would now alter these things. We would obtain for women the right to such academical honours as would afford a sufficient motive and stimulus for thorough, accurate, and sustained study by young women past mere girlhood, and able to acquire the higher branches of knowledge. This *general* and great benefit would be the first object—the raising for *all* women the standard of education. But, beside this general utility, we believe that great special use would accrue to certain classes of women (and through them to the community) from thus opening to them the benefit of University education.

First, as regards those intending to be governesses. Here will be first provided an exceedingly high standard, held out with due encouragements for those who seek the chief places in the profession. An entirely new class of instructresses will, we believe, be thence created. Secondly, mothers, whether themselves well taught or ignorant, will know on what they depend when they engage such governesses; and not, as now, find themselves constantly deceived by shallow pretence, and references to ill-judging employers. Thirdly, and above all, a few dozen *accurately* trained governesses would, I am convinced, do much to revolutionize the present state of female education in the country, by giving to their pupils the same habits of solid and accurate study they have themselves acquired. The slovenly lessons, the half-corrected exercises, will then, we hope, be at an end; and the young lady's schoolroom become a mental gymnasium, where health and soundness of mind will be gained for life, instead of what it now is too often—a place where ineradicable habits are acquired of mental scrambling and shuffling, of shallowness and false show. And again, these certificates will be of importance as preliminary steps to the introduction of women into the medical profession. On this great subject I have no space worthily to speak, and can therefore only refer to it as one of the improvements most to be desired. Such little experience as I have myself had of such matters has lain among a class the most piteous assuredly in the community—the sufferers from incurable disease. I can only record my conviction that a large number of women among them would have been saved from agonizing deaths had they been able in the first stages of their disorder to obtain the advice of female doctors. There are other employments beside those of governesses and physicians—clerkships, secretaryships, and the like, to which the admission of women will be universally facilitated by the proposed degrees. These matters are, however, sufficiently obvious to require no discussion.

I hope I have now in some measure demonstrated—first, that some improvement is needed in the condition of young women, and that a better education is one of the stages of such improvement. Secondly, that a high education does not make women *less* able and willing to perform their natural duties, but better and more intelligently able and willing to do so. Thirdly, that to assimilate the *forms* of a woman's education to that of a man by means of examinations and academical honours, and also the *substance* of it by means of classical and mathematical studies, will in nowise tend to efface the natural differences of their minds, which depend not on any accidental circumstances, to be regulated by education, but on innate characteristics given by the Creator. Fourthly, that there are many positive benefits, general and particular, to be expected from such Examinations and Honours, such classical and mathematical studies being opened to women.

Now it happens that there is one institution in this country which seems especially qualified to afford the advantages we have supposed—namely, the London University. In the older Universities the rule of collegiate residence necessarily excludes women; but in London, the examinations being open to all, wheresoever educated, there is no reason why young ladies studying in the various female colleges, or in their homes, should not be admitted to share all the benefits of the institution.

As most of my readers are no doubt aware, the proposal that women should be thus admitted has been lately under debate in the Senate of the University—the occasion of a new charter offering a convenient opportunity for the change. A clause (it was suggested) should be inserted, extending the present terms, "all classes and denominations of her Majesty's subjects, without any exception whatever," to that *small* class, including half the human race, to which her Majesty herself belongs. This proposition, after much debate, was negatived, but only by the casting-vote of the chairman. Not unreasonably, therefore, may we hope that on the next occasion a fresh consideration will be given to the case, and another decision obtained. That so startling a proposal received on its first suggestion the votes of ten members of the Senate out of twenty, is much more surprising than that it should have been ultimately rejected. The long list of eminent names which has been obtained in favour of the movement, is guarantee for an amount of public opinion which may well inspire confidence in eventual success.

Should it so prove, and the University of London open its doors to women, the time will not be far distant when the innovation, which some may now regard as a derogation from its dignity, will be boasted of as no inconsiderable claim to public gratitude and respect. Those inequalities of the two sexes which place women at a disadvantage during ages when might makes right, are altered in happier times, when the strong heart is seen to be worth as much as the strong head. The tide has turned for women, and by and by the credit of helping their progress will not be lightly esteemed. Even were this otherwise, however, the University of London would hardly suffer, I think, from following in the course of the schools of Alexandria, where the martyr Hypatia held the first chair of philosophy then existing in the world; or in that of the University of Padua, where women learned and taught by the side of Galileo, Petrarch, and Columbus.

In conclusion, I would venture to make one appeal: do not let us in this, or any other matter connected with women's claims, allow ourselves to be drawn aside by those prejudices which on both sides distract us. To a woman of refined feeling, that popular Ogress, the Strong-minded Female, is so distasteful, that she is inclined rather to leave her whole sex to mental starvation than contribute to the sustenance of one specimen of the genus. To a man with a spark of fun in his composition, the temptation to perpetrate jokes about Mistresses of Arts and Spinsters of Arts is perfectly irresistible. But, after all, refined women will best prevent the growth of strong-mindedness, in its obnoxious sense, by bringing their own good taste to help their sisters, whom the harsh struggles of life under a woman's disadvantages have perhaps somewhat hardened and embittered. And men who laugh at the absurdities (incident, alas! in some mysterious way to all the doings of women), will also in graver moments feel that there is another side to the subject, not a ludicrous one; and that the answer of the poor frogs to the boys in the fable might often be made by human sufferers: "throwing stones may be fun to you, but it is death to us." To aid a woman in distress was deemed in the old days of chivalry the chiefest honour of the bravest knight; it is assuredly no less an honour now for wise and generous men to aid the whole sex to a better and nobler life, and to the developing more perfectly, because more fully and freely, that Womanhood which God has also made in His own image—a divine and holy thing.

THE END.

For EU product safety concerns, contact us at Calle de José Abascal, 56–1°,
28003 Madrid, Spain or eugpsr@cambridge.org.

www.ingramcontent.com/pod-product-compliance
Ingram Content Group UK Ltd.
Pitfield, Milton Keynes, MK11 3LW, UK
UKHW010339140625
459647UK00010B/711